AF646443

Dimensions of Physical Education

Edited & Compiled by

Dr. Anil Sharma

KHEL SAHITYA KENDRA
7/26, Ansari Road, Darya Ganj,
New Delhi-110002.

Published by:

KHEL SAHITYA KENDRA

7/26, Ansari Road, Darya Ganj, New Delhi-110002.

Ph.: (O) 011-65190343, 43551324, 42564726
(M) 9811088729, (Fax) 011-42564726, (Res.) 47091605

E-mail: *khelsahitya1@rediffmail.com*

Web: *www.khelsahitya.com*

© 2012 Publisher

I.S.B.N. - 978-81-7524-616-4

PRINTED IN INDIA 2012

All Rights Reserved.

No part of this publication may be stored in a retrieval system, transmitted or reproduced in any way, including but not limited to photocopy, photograph, magnetic or other record, without the prior agreement and written permission of the publisher.

Laser Typeset by:

JAIN MEDIA GRAPHICS
Delhi-110035.

Printed by:

ASIAN OFFSET PRINTERS
Delhi

Price: Rs. 750/-

Contents

1

EDUCATION AND PHYSICAL EDUCATION—AN INTRODUCTION

What is Education?

Education in the largest sense is any act or experience that has a formative effect on the mind, character or physical ability of an individual. In its technical sense, education is the process by which society deliberately transmits its accumulated knowledge, skills and values from one generation to another.

Education is the process of development which consists of the passage of the human being from infancy to maturity and, the process whereby he adapts himself gradually in various ways to his physical social and spiritual environment. But even in this social process, the child needs support and freedom from an economic pressure, and that is why education requires long period of social as well as biological infancy when the young would live off the labour of others and be released from self support. However, assistance will be at least partially discounted unless education at the same time encourages wise and discriminating consumption. The child should bot become a parasite. He must pay back by realising the goals and objectives that education sets for him upto his optimal capacity, sincerity and honestly.

Education must focus on total and optimal development of human resource.

Teachers in educational institutions direct the education of students and might draw on many subjects, including reading, writing, mathematics, science and history. This process is sometimes called schooling when referring to the education of teaching only a certain subject, usually as professors at institutions of higher learning. There is also education in fields for those who want specific vocational skills, such as those required to be a pilot. In addition there is an array of education possible at the informal level, such as in museums and libraries, with the Internet and in life experience. Many non-traditional education options are now available and continue to evolve.

Various experts have defined the concept of education differently. For instance, Prof. Drever has defined it as a process with the help of which one can give a proper shape to the knowledge, character and behaviour of someone. In other words, education is a constructive process which can lead to enlightenment and can develop various aspects of an individual's personality. With the help of proper education, there can be physical development, mental development and social development also. Another expert, P.C. Banerji has said that education helps in developing the power of adaptation to an ever changing social environment. Thus one thing Banerji has made clear is that nature and outlook of society keeps on changing, and society is being made by people living in it and outlook of society changes when the nature of behaviour of people living in it change. Kant has stated that education is an important development in an individual of all the perfections of which he is capable.

Thus, it can be said that education results in an integrated, balanced and all-round development of an individual, which can help him in becoming a civilised and responsible member of the society. Education provides a man dynamic personality which provide him maturity and help him in becoming a more maturer person.

Definition of Education

1. According to Socrates, "Education means the bringing out the ideas of universal validity which are in the mind of every man."

2. According to Mahatma Gandhi ji, "By education I means an all round drawing out of the best in child and man: body, mind and soul.

3. According to Freobel, "Education is process by which child makes his internal external."

4. Other, "Education is the manifestation of perfection already reached in man."

Systems of Formal Education

Education is a concept, referring to the process in which students can learn something:

- Instruction refers to the facilitating of learning toward identified objectives, delivered either by an instructor or other forms.

- Learning refers to learning with a view toward preparing learners with specific knowledge, skills, or abilities that can be applied immediately upon completion.

Importance of Education

Education is important from various points of view. Its field of activity is so wide that all activities and experience are embraced in tis sphere of work. Essentially, it is process of development, a development of the latent, inherent capacities of a child to the fullest extent. It sublimates the animal basic instincts in a child to socially useful activities, habits of thinking and behaving. It inculcate values, so that he is able to form a strong character useful to his own self and to the society of which he is an internal part. Further, education meets the immediate needs of a child and also social and refined patterns of behaviour. Not only this, is develops all his intellectual and emotional powers, so that he is able to meet the problems of life squarely and solve them successfully. It also develops the social qualities of service, tolerance, co-operation, fellow-feeling, inspiring the child to lay down all, even his life, for the glory and prosperity of his country. Last but not the least, education infuses in the child a spirit of dynamic citizenship which eggs him on in the service of his nation keeping in consideration the international understanding and well-being of humanity as a whole.

Aims and Objectives of Education

The importance of aims and objectives of education is recognised by all the educational, professional, political, nonpolitical and religious associations, organisations and groups at various levels in their memoranda, letters and brouchures. It is said that education without clear cut aims is like a rudderless ship.

Education, suggested in the documents, include individual as well as social aims, with emphasis of social transformation aiming at reconstructing society to make it modernised, productive, partidipative, and value oriented nation committed to its constitutional obligations.

1. Individual Development

Development of an individual - physically, mentally and spritually is well known aim of education. Objectives related to this aim of individual development have been expressed in various ways in the memoranda:

- Developing physical and mental faculties

- Acquiring the capacities of understanding, appreciation and expression through word and act, are the fundamental aims of education

- Aim of education should be to make children self-confident and self dependent, and to make them strong physically and mentally

- Education is meant to develop every child's character, personality and culture and as much knowledge as the child can assimilate not merely memorize.

The best expression of complete development of an individual and the harmonious development of personality, however, is found in the following paragraph.

The policy should be directed to the aim of enlightenment of head and heart; illumination of consciousness for allround development of individual personality. Education should enable a human being to attain the greatest possible harmony, internal and external, spiritual and material, for the fullest possible development of human potentialities and capacities.

2. Social and National Development

Social, aim of education in equally important because an individual lives in society and has his obligations towards his nation. There is a realisation that, "The present education system does riot yield required results mainly because it is divorced from the real social content and social goals".

It has, therefore, been suggested that education should be able, to discharge its natural functions and must correspond to its structure, goals and content in the interest of national development and social progress. It has also been suggested in this connection that students from young age should be made aware of the social responsibility cast on them.

At the same time, there are certain constitutional commitments, which are intimately related to this aim.. We as the citizens of the republic, are constitutionally Committed to democracy, social justice, equality of opportunity, secularism and above all to a welfare state. It has, therefore, been suggested that, "Educational policy and educational programme should clearly reflect these commitments".

3. Social Transformation

Education should not merely equip an individual to adjust with society to its customs and conventions, but it should enable him to bring desirable changes in the society. It has been, therefore, suggested that, "Every educational institution from secondary school to university college should be developed to become an agency of change...."

However, it is essential that we should be quite clear about the purpose of change. It is, therefore, natural to ask the, question, "Reform and change to achieve what"? What type of society we aim at and what type of citizens we wish to produce? The following ideas give an indication of the kind of changes education is expected to bring about.

3.1 Modernisation

Modernisation of society in terms of scientific and technological advancement is a view which seems to be quite popular. It is though that education should enable us to move with times and attain excellence in, science and technology. To quote an expression of this kind.

Scientific and technological advances are, gaining momentum and conscious efforts are made to incorporate them into the development sectors. This calls for modernisation of education in order to make. It in conformity with the modern times and to keep pace, with the advances in the world.

3.2 Productivity

Some documents have insisted on linking education with productivity and thus making individuals as productive citizens to build a productive society. One of the suggestions, in a memorandum, for example, says. "It should bring about a social transformation, and enhance greater efficiency and productivity in all sectors : agri- cultural, industrial and service". It is in this context that Mahatma Gandhi's system of basic education is still considered as a basically sound system and a suggestion has been made that with necessary modification elements of basic education may form part of education not only at the primary stage but at all stages in our national system of education.

3.3 Community Participation

In a democracy education without community

participation is barren. This aim of education is, therefore voiced by a number of groups and organisations. The change that is envisaged on this front is that of Integrating education with community in all respects.

4. Acquisition of Values

Moral, cultural and spiritual values in education have been given immense importance in the Memoranda documents. One of the expressions emphatically point out that, "certain basic values as respect for others, responsibility, solidarity, creativity and integrity must be fostered in our children".

5. Summing up

It is worth reproducing what a document mentions about the aims of education:

The aim of education is two-fold (i) Development of the individual in society and (ii) Consequent development of the society. The aim of education in relation to individual may be spelt out as follows:

i) to produce full human personality with courage, conviction, vitality, sensitivity and intelligence so that men and women may life in harmony with the universe;

ii) to bring out the fullest potential of child and prepare him for life and its varied situations so that he becomes a cultured and responsible citizen dedicated in the service of community.

In relation to the society, the aim of education is to create:

i) a sane and learning society where made of material production will be such that no section of the society remains unemployed. In the Indian context such a made of production will be necessarily based on a decentralised economy utilising all available manpower;

ii) a society. where the conditions of work and general environment will offer psychic satisfactions and effective motivations to its members.

iii) a society reconciling technological and scientific advancement with general well-being and security of its members, enhancing joy of life and eliminating all forms of exploitation.

The broad objective of education should, therefore, be to look beyond the existing society and to develop men and women amenable to the advent of a sane and healthier society of tomorrow.

Different Aspects of Education

It is not an easy task to define the word education as it is very broad in nature. Education provides a precise meaning. Education has a very complicated nature as it deals with human beings and human beings have an ever progressive nature. Moreover, the society in which human beings live is also keeps on changing and in this kind of condition, it is really not easy to provide a proper definition of concept of Education.

According to the different life situations, definition of concept of education keeps on changing. There are various theories dealing with the origin of concept of education. According to one theory, word education has been derived from a Latin word Educere which implies to lead out and to bring forth. On the basis of the word from where word education is being derived, some experts define it as a means to lead out a human being and to bring forth or develop the abilities he possess. Whatever one man possess inside him, i.e., knowledge, power, ability, it is with the help of education that can be bring out or can be developed.

According to another school of experts, the word education has been derived from a Latin word 'Education' which is formed of two distinct words, namely, 'e' and 'duco'. In literal sense, word 'e' implies out of and word 'duco' implies to lead out. When these two words combine with each other, the concept that emerges out is a process which helps in developing one's inner abilities or which brings out the inner capabilities of a human being.

There lies some inner capacities, which are there in a human being right from the birth. This capability is termed as the innate capacity to learn. This capacity can also be developed with the help of education. It can be said that education is such a process which result in a progressive and systematic development of man's all inner abilities. Process of education is continuous in nature. In other words, it is a never ending process. It can be viewed as a progress and development which cannot be stopped.

Goals of Education

General Education enhances students' ability to:

1. Think critically and analytically integrate and synthesize knowledge, and draw conclusions from complex material.

2. Make sound ethical and value judgements based on the development of a personal value system, on an understanding of shared culture heritage, and knowledge of past success, failures, and consequences of individual roles and societal choices.

3. Understand and appreciate the culture diversity of the U.S. and other countries, and live responsibly in an interdependent world.

4. Acquire a base of knowledge common to educated persons and the capacity to expand that base over their lifetime.

5. Communicate effectively in written, oral, and symbolic form

6. Understand the nature and physical world, the process by which scientific concepts are developed and modified.

7. Appreciate the fine and performing arts.

8. Develop the mathematical and quantitative skills necessary of calculation, analysis and problem solving.

9. Understand the principles essential for continual mental and physical well-being.

The final output which is being got from the process of education is termed as its objective. Around a centre of purpose, an objective revolves. It is abstract in nature and can never realized fully. Process of education should be such that it can provide a kind of challenge to teachers and students as well. It should have the power to inspire towards greater effort.

Objective of education can be considered a hub of wheel, around which all other aims of education revolve or lie. It can be compared to a thread that can bring all valid objectives of education into an integrated form. Various experts have provided their views on the objectives of education, some of which are as follows :—

According to Swami Vivekanada : A perfect man making should be the objective of all kinds of education. Education, with the help of which character can be formed, strength of mind can be increased and intellect can be expanded should be taught.

According to Gandhi Ji : Education which can draw out and stimulate the spiritual, intellectual and physical faculties of the children should be considered a true education.

To deal with various issues or aspects relating to education in our country, an commission, with the name Secondary Education Commission was set up in the year 1952-53. The commission has mentioned four main objectives of education in India. According to the list provided by this commission, objectives of education include the following :—

a. Improvement of vocational efficiency,

b. Development of democratic citizenship,

c. Development of qualities for leadership, and

d. Development of personality.

In 1986, a New Policy of Education was prepared, in which goals of the education were mentioned very clearly. According to this policy, major goals of education are the following :—

a. To achieve an overall development of an individual with the help of integrated programme of education, and

b. To make education system such that it can play an important role in process of development of nation.

Meaning and Definition of Physical Education

The word physical refers to body, and indicates bodily characteristics such as strength, speed, endurance, flexibility, health coordination and performance. It seemingly contrasts the body with the mind. The term education when used in conjunction with physical, refers to a process of education that develops the human body especially fitness and movement skills. Therefore, it transcends all misconceptions and misgivings about physical education as a field of teaching and being considered as an ingredient of general education.

A bird's eye-view of various definitions of physical education is essential. Physical Education as understood is such a cultivation of power and capabilities of student as will enable him to maintain his bodily condition in the best working order providing at the same time for the greater efficiency of his intellectual and spiritual life. It is proclaimed that physical education should aim to improve the mass of students and to give them as much health, strength and stamina as possible to enable them to perform the duties that await them after they leave their college."

These early definitions, laid emphasis on (i) the development of physical qualities which enable the individual to live his life successfully and efficiently and (ii) the process which is essentially educational in perspective.

Physical Education is rightly recognized as an integral part of education. The existence of man is primarily physical. The first lessons a human child learns are lessons of physical activity. No education, howsoever ideal and exalted in its objectives, is complete without emphasis on motor activity. The human body is a sacred gift of Nature. Its growth, development and efficiency largely depends upon the quantity and quality of motor activities it performs. Compartmentalization of human personality into "body, mind, and spirit" is an over-simplification.

The mind and spirit do not reveal themselves

without body. The body, being an observable material cause of mind, is an instrument through which man performs all mundane duties enjoined upon him by Nature and society.

From an overview of various definitions the following salient features of physical education emerge:

1. Physical education is essentially education for it is a means through which body, soul and intellect get moving—efficiently and vigorously.
2. In physical education, the main stress is "big muscle" or "large muscle" activity—an innate quality of the human organism. No wholesome experience is derived unless activity programmes are selective as well as elective and imbibe values other than physical alone.
3. The worthy outcomes shall accrue only when the individual participates in the activity programme. Nobody can learn to swim unless he gets into water.
4. The physical, mental, intellectual, spiritual, and social aspects of a "wholesome" personality are interrelated. Physical education strives to maintain and strengthen the body-mind spirit integration.
5. No where do the aim and objectives of physical education come in conflict with the objectives of education. In fact, they are like hand in glove.
6. Physical education is the only unique discipline which uses "physical activity" as the medium for human development. Its approach to its objectives is natural and unambiguous.

Aims and Objectives of Physical Education

The aims and objectives of physical education depend to a great extent on the political, economic and social changes that take place in a society.

* The development of organic fitness.

* The development of neuromuscular skill.

* The development of character and personality.

* To prepare highly qualified leaders in the field of physical education and sports.

Opportunities Galore :

Don't think that a career in sports field is only that of sweating it out on the play field. There are many lucrative and well paying technical as well as other jobs beckoning sports people today.

Career as a coach or a physical education instructor is the main option in the field. Their job entails selecting potential players and then teaching them the rules of the game, demonstrate various techniques, ways to plan a game and devise strategy.

They also observe players and offer them guidance and helpful criticism. They accompany players for competitions and motivate them so as to bring out the best in them.

Pursuing an additional post - graduate diploma in physical training can enable one to find expert jobs as physiotherapists or lecturers at a university) both in India and abroad.

One can also join one of the many health centres that are opening in clubs and hotels as fitness experts and have a respectable job and a handsome pay package.

Experienced coaches are in great demand at all the training centres set up by SAI and by state and central sports bodies.

Besides sports clubs, schools and colleges, they can also work as in - house coaches for corporate sports teams.

Physical Education should aim to provide a skilled kind of leadership and necessary facilities, which can provide an opportunity to the individual or group to behave or act in according to the conditions which are mentally stimulating and socially sound. There should be better opportunities that can be provided.

Various experts have provided their views relating to the aims of physical education, some of which are as follows :—

In the words of J.R. Sherman : The fundamental goal of physical education is to affect the experiences of individual to the extent that each individual can help to adjust successfully in changing conditions, which will result an increase in his desires, and develop the ability to fulfil his wants.

In the words of Bookwalters : The goal of physical education is proper and all-round development of a human being with the help of some guided instructions and by the use of various kinds of activities which should be conducted in accordance with the needs and social standards.

According to Nixon and Cozen : Physical education should have a goal of making the maximum contribution to the development of an individual's potentialities in all areas of life which can be done by placing him in an environment to promote such muscular and related responses as will contribute to this purpose successfully.

Thus it can be said that the main goal of physical education is to develop of personality of an individually in such a way that he can live comfortably and successfully in the changed environment and conditions.

Fundamental Objectives of Physical Education

The means which are being used to realize the goals are called objectives. It can be said that objectives are advances and steps which relate to the goals. They do an important function of measuring up to the standards of the goals and because of this reason they are considered very important and worthwhile.

Objectives are those weapons which can help in bringing set aims or goals upto the realisation point. Objectives are desirable and they seem possible of being realised.

Various experts have provided different objectives of physical education, some of which are as follows :—

a. Development of health and physique of the individual.

b. Mental or emotional development of the individual.

c. Development of neuro-muscular capabilities.

d. Development of physical efficiency and also to maintain it throughout the life.

e. Development of some important and useful skills.

f. To help individual to learn efficiently in physical activities and also to perform actively in other activities of life.

Scope of Physical Education

Physical education is a very developed area and it has a very wide scope. Today, it is not mere limited to various kinds of physical exercises. All the factors or activities which help in developing an individual's personality are included in it now. It consists of all the areas or facets of human activities.

Now, knowledge of physical education or participation in physical activities are not concerned important only for the school going students, but now it is recognised important for people of all ages and both the sex. Whatever the physical abilities of individuals, all the persons should participate in different kinds of physical activities. The objective of physical education programmes is not only to train or create outstanding players, but another important objective it has is to maintain the health of all the people using or participating in it.

Today, programmes of physical education are prepared in such a way that needs and requirements of all the people get fulfilled. According to the age and requirements of people participating in the activities, one should prepare the programme carefully. Various kinds of programmes can be prepared, some of which are Service Programme, Intramural and Extramural Programme and Fitness and Recreational Programme. The programme in which importance is provided to the instructional aspect is termed as service programme. Such programme in which provide opportunities to develop the skills and abilities to all the participants is termed as intramural programme.

Need and Importance of Physical Education in Modern Era

In the Present World of Space age and automation era, all human beings appear to be living a more and more inactive life. They ride instead of walk, sit instead of stand and watches instead of participants. Such type of inactivity or sedentary life is detrimental to mental and physical health. Thus, there is great need for physical education as a part of balanced living.

Following are the importance or benefits of physical education -

1. It is needed because due to advanced technology the lifestyle of people becomes sedentary and they become passive entertainer.

2. It is needed during childhood for proper growth and development.

3. It is beneficial during adulthood to maintain good health and fitness.

4. During old Age, it is important to prevent and treat various ailments and disease.

5. It is important as it provides us the knowledge of our bodies from musculoskeletal, physiological and biochemical point of view.

6. It teaches us various physical activities that can be practiced now in later life such as motor skills for the games and sports of volleyball, tennis, swimming and so on.

7. It also teaches us the value of ethical behaviour in sporting situations.

8. It teaches us the value of physical fitness and how to become physically fit.

Relationship Between Physical Education and General Education

Physical Education holds an important position in modern educational system. No doubt, complete development is impossible without a sound body. General Education and Physical Education is also important from national and social point of view. Our youth cannot be steered towards the pursuit of national development till this subject of General Education and Physical Education is properly taught in our school. Man is an indivisible integration comprising body, mind and spirit. Attempt to drive a wedge between the bodily functions and mental processes would be an exercise in futility because the organism acts and reacts as a whole and not in parts. The age-old myth that body and mind are separate entities has since been exploded. While the body is considered as the gross, concrete and solid aspect of the universal matter, mind and spirit represent its fine, ethereal and celestial qualities. Soul without body, mind without matter and education without 'movement' are meaningless concepts.

A properly directed physical education should result in health, happiness, efficiency and character. The physical welfare of youth of the country should be one of the main concerns of state and any departure from the normal standards of physical well being at this period of life may have serious consequences. According to the law of Nature, the first lesson of education a child learns, is the lesson of "body movement". Movement is the basis of growth and development. The development of neuro-muscular system is a prerequisite to perceptual and cognitive development. Therefore, the primacy of 'movement education'—informal or formal—in the orbit of education is well-established. Eduction may mean different things to different people but the essence of all definitions of education is that it should afford equal opportunities to all for optimal development of their potential. It should draw out the best in child. This broad-based and comprehensive view of education takes cognizance of all the factors that contribute to the harmonious development of human personality. The development of brain without corresponding development of the brawn is hazardous.

Therefore, the importance of physical education as a core curricular activity must be recognized. Both education and physical education are doing phenomena. Modern educationists do not subscribe to "knowledge-acquisition" as the sole purpose of education. Rather stress is laid on "learning by doing". Physical education is an activity-oriented endeavour the main thrust of which is on "doing and learning". Activity is a binding buckle between education and physical education. The classroom academic activity and physical activity on the play-field must compliment and supplement each other for the balanced growth of human personality. Play-fields, gymnasia, stadia etc., are the temples and laboratories of physical education where children receive practical training of life.

Bucher set four major objectives of education. Specifying a variety of goals and sub-goals under these objectives, he vouched that physical education must play a significant role in helping children achieve them.

The objectives of civic responsibility involve humanitarianism, tolerance, conformance to laws, civic responsibility and democratic living. Playing games necessarily requires participants to be obedient, to conform to rules and regulations of the game, to act as responsible members of the team and follow thee principles of democratic living. Sportsmanship and sportsman's spirit are always referred to as the most cherished qualities of an amiable personality. Physical education must purge the individual and the society of negative feelings, pent-up emotions and destructive tendencies which often cause political upheavals and social turmoils.

The objectives of self-realization include an enquiring mind, knowledge of health and diseases, family and community health, skill as a participant and spectator, utilizing leisure in mental pursuits and appreciation of beauty. Organized physical education cuticula should afford opportunities to all sorts of people to (1) actively explore and interact with the social and physical environment. (2) know their physical and mental capabilities, strengths and weaknesses. (3) acquire knowledge about personal, family and community health. (4) learn how to be competitors and spectators.

The objectives of economic efficiency entail good workmanship, vocational placement, successful work, professional growth and wise consumption of goods and services. Doubts are sometimes expressed as to the direct link of these goals of education with physical education. The reality is that physical education ensures a very high degree of health and fitness in the participants. Production and productivity—the main props of economic efficiency—cannot be increased without health and fitness of the masses. Physical education, in fact, indirectly contributes to these educational objectives. By offering myriad avenue for vocational placement to participants and athletes, physical education helps people improve their economic status. Outstanding sports-persons can undergo suitable vocational courses to serve as physical educators, coaches, sports administrators, managers, sports scientists, sports journalists and the like. Physically-educated persons must also learn how to be economical in the expenditure of their energy and use of goods and services. Only fit and healthy people can ensure a nation's economic efficiency and professional growth.

The objectives of human relationship refer to human welfare in general and that of participants in particular, rich social experience, cooperation, courtesy, fairness and sportsmanship, family welfare and home-living. Physical education must ensure human welfare, and provide recreation which is an antidote to such vices as apartheid, aggression, political vendetta etc. Sports, games, and adventurous activities like mountaineering, rock-climbing, sky-diving, marathon racing etc., may be highly competitive, challenging and risky in nature but not devoid of humanistic approach to global problems. Play-fields should be a leveller of inequalities—racial, social, lingual and economic. Play activities must result in a rich and abundant social experience which underscores such qualities as co-operation, co-existence, fair play, courtesy, obedience, sportsmanship, honesty, spirit of tolerance etc. Practice but not preaching, example but not precept should be thee guiding principles on thee play-field. The players must learn to play the game in the spirit of thee game, transcending all barriers of caste, creed, religion and status. The Olympic Games were revived with the sole objective of creating international understanding and human brotherhood.

Various kinds of social and cultural values are being aroused in players by participating in physical activities. They not only develop physically but also mentally. By participating in sports, ability to judge and to take proper decisions in shortest time becomes possible. Qualities of loyalty, co-operation and co-ordination aroused in human beings, which help them in developing their personality to a lot of extent, which is also an important objective of education.

In this way, it is observed that the basic objectives of education get fulfilled by physical education because of which physical education is considered an important and indispensable area of education. In today's modern society, there exists a strong relationship between general education and physical education. These two kinds of education are not substitutes of each other, but are supplementary in nature. One without other cannot achieve its objectives. Physical education should be considered an important part of general education and it should be provided proper place in education curriculum.

Modern Trends in Physical Education

To promote various kinds of sports activities in our country, government of India or various regional sports organisations establish various kinds of sports schemes from time to time. Not only this, for encouraging people to participate in sports activities, various organisations and institutions are also established by government or by private individuals where they can get coaching or training of different kinds of activities. In this chapter, point of our focus will be various kinds of schemes which are being prepared by government of India and the institutions which are owned by government authorities and the private authorities.

One of an important sports coaching scheme is Raj Kumari Amrit Kaur Sports Coaching Scheme. When the

National Stadium situated in New Delhi and Vallabhabhai Patel Stadium in Bombay were constructed, the then union minister thought to use the facilities provided by these stadiums in such a way that they could help in improving the sports standards in our country. In the year 1952, union minister approached the then prime minister with a project for organising sports coaching in our country. Pandit Jawahar Lal Nehru, who was the prime minister at that time, liked the project and sanctioned around Rs. 75000 for the same. It was in the 1953 that the project was launched in reality. The main objective of the scheme was to provide players or sportspeople with various kinds of technical assistance that can enable them to grow to the maximum extent. To achieve this objective, Central government supported the scheme whole heartedly.

With a period of four years, various positive results were being got from the scheme. Scheme helped in fulfilling the requirement of sports coaching as an important necessity for sustained performance in various kinds of competitions. The requirement for continued governmental subsidy and patronage to keep this programme going in the future years was also got fulfilled.

One of the brightest and important year for the Raj Kumari Amrit Kaur Coaching Scheme was 1955-56. It was during this year that various foreign coaches and players visited India. Various top class players of the world encouraged to use this scheme. Morale of the Indian players increased to a great extent and horizon of Indian coaches widened to a lot of extent. It was in the year that some permanent coaching schools were being established in two metropolitan cities, namely, the Delhi and Bombay. To provide more attention on school and college athletes in these cities, additional coaches were being employed. It was because of this scheme, that in a large number, outstanding coaches came into being.

In the financial year 1956-57, central government rose its grant to 4 lakhs. After this, the scheme's prime objective became to cover needs and requirements of players of school and college levels. To fulfil the demands of school and colleges in the country, more coaches were being employed. Services of foreign coaches were employed to the minimum extent. By saving money through employment of Indian coaches, more funds could be used for organising various kinds of camps at different parts of the country. The emphasis shifted to schools and colleges. Organisation of various kinds of tournament for different sections of the society also became an important part of the objectives of the scheme. It was with the result of using this scheme that it was realised that coaching play an important role in the field of games and sports.

As mentioned earlier that to promote sports activities in the country, various private and government owned institutions are being set up, which provide training to the players relating to various sports. Some of such institutions are as follows :—

Sports Authority of India (SAI)

Successor organisation of ninth Asian games which were held in the year 1982 in New Delhi, is Sports Authority of India. This authority was established in the form of a society which was being registered under the Registration of Societies Act, 1860, on 1984. Promotion of games and sports in the country was the main objective of establishing this authority.

It was very necessary to maintain the utilize the existing stadiums in Delhi, which were being constructed during the ninth Asian games, and for this purpose, an authority was being set up with the name of Sports Authority of India. In 1987, Society for National Institutes of Physical Education and Sports was being emerged with this Sports Authority of India the purpose of which was to perform the function of promotion and development of Sports awareness among the people of India with efficiency. In promoting various sports activities in the country, this authority has played a very important role. Prime Minister is appointed as the president of this authority. Union minister for human resource development is assign the task of heading the governing body of authority. On the post of vice chairperson, union minister of the state for youth affairs and sports is appointed.

As per the rules of this authority, it is necessary for the general body to meet atleast once in a year while the governing body is required to meet atleast for once in each quarter of the financial year. Any member secretary of the general body is appointed as the secretary of the authority. Govt. of India reconstituted the general and governing body of this authority in the year 1998. Now, prime minister will be assigned the post of ex-officio president of the general body of the authority.

Main Aims of Sports Authority of India

Sports Authority of India has been set-up with some specific objectives, some of which are as follows :—

a. Implementation of the existing schemes is one of an important objective of this authority. Only those schemes which are designed with an objective of promoting the sports and improving the standards of sports in the country are being taken into consideration in this scheme.

b. Promotion and development of sports activities is another objective of this scheme. While keeping the view the sports policy of the government of India, it is also an objective to make use of various plans which are designed to promote the standard of sports in our country.

c. To sponsor and encourage people to conduct various kinds of research works which are being done with the objective of bringing developments in the sports and games.

d. To construct and utilise various kinds of residential facilities for players and other persons which are engaged with sports in some way.

e. Planning, developing and utilising various kinds of facilities and infrastructure which are necessary for conducting sports events.

f. Construction of various centres where training relating to various sports events can be provided.

g. To make provision of various kinds of essential assistance which are required to organise championships or tournaments at various levels.

Constituents of Governing and General Body

Governing Body : There should be 28 members in the governing body out of which govt. of India nominates 16 members, while the rest 12 members are ex-officio members.

General Body : This body should be consisted of 43 members. Out of these 43 members, 27 are non-official members and 16 are ex-officio members. Non-official members of the body are being appointed by Indian Government.

Functions performed by Sports Authority of India

In various functional wings, function of sports authority of India can be categorise. Each wing is being headed by an Executive Director. Generally, this authority is being divided into following wings :—

a. Academic Wing,

b. Team Wing,

c. Operations Wing,

d. Stadia Wings,

All these wings perform different kind of functions, the information relating to each wing is as follows :—

a. Academic Wing : This wing is further divided into two other wings, under the names of Academic Wings for Physical Education and Academic Wing for sports.

Academic Wings for Physical Education — This wing is known as Lakshmibai National College of Physical Education, which is being situated in Trivandrum. It was in the year 1985 that government of India established this college. The objective of establishing this college was to provide various kinds of sports facilities which are required for the upliftment or improvement of standard of physical education and sports in our country. To the university of Kerala, this college is being affiliated. By passing out from this college, one can get bachelor as well as master's degree in physical education. Bachelor degree has a duration of three years, while the time duration of master's degree is two years.

Academic Wing for Sports — This wing is located in

Patiala. Generally, it is called Sports Academy of India Netaji Subhash National Institute of Sports. Various kinds of facilities are being offered by this wing, some of which are as follow :—

i. For training sports persons in coaching, diploma courses are provided in this college, which have a duration of one year.

ii. Master's course in sports coaching is being provided, which have a duration of two years.

iii. Diploma courses in sports medicine are offered by this college, which have a duration of two years.

iv. This college provides the international Olympic committee solidarity courses, which are being conducted from time to time.

v. For physical education teachers or coach, this college offers a certificate course in sports, which have a duration of six weeks.

b. Team Wing : Directorate of Teams, Equipment Support and Dope control lab are the constituents of this wing. It is necessary to discuss all the constituents separately, which is done as under :—

Directorate of Equipment support : All kinds of equipments required for training players of national teams are arranged or imported by this directorate. Rate contrary to various sports equipments are being finalised by these directorates. To various national and international competitions, different sports equipments are being provided on the loan basis by this directorate.

Directorate of Teams : The responsibility for long term training of selected sports persons lie with the directorate of teams. It is the duty of this directorate to train player in such a way that they can perform well in various kinds of competitions. This director also deal the matters relating to the deployment of foreign coaches or visit by foreign experts for providing training to the national teams. This wing provide training facilities, boarding and lodging and sports equipment and in this way play a supportive role in promoting various sports events in the country.

Dope Control Directorate : This directorate is being situated in Jawahar Lal Nehru stadium. The main function performed by this directorate is to ensure that no player is taking or consuming those drugs the use of which have been banned by organisation and considered to be an illegal act.

c. Operations Wing : Director of Sports Promotion in Education Sector and Special Area Games and Infrastructure are included in this wing. The main objective or function of these directorates is to nurture young children with required talent in different age groups, which the help of various means. An important function of directorate of infrastructure is to monitor the progress of various kinds of capital works. Under the various schemes, the talented children are being spotted at the optimum age level in different discipline are provided with scientific training at the various centres of scheme, with the objective of achieving excellence at the National and Junior International levels.

Netaji Subhash National Institute of Sports, Patiala (NSNIS)

The performance of Indian players remained very poor in the third Asian Games, which were being held in 1958. In the hockey, performance of Indian players remained very low. Pakistan defeated Indian team very badly. Indian hockey lovers and government of India got a kind of shock with the defeat of his team in the game of hockey. To enquire about the reasons of defeat of Indian team, an ad-hoc enquiry committee was being set up in 1958 by the government of India. This committee was also entrusted to provide the suggestions which can could be implemented to improve the adverse condition of hockey team. Maharaja Yadvindra Singh of Patiala was appointed as the chairman of the committee.

Suggestion to establish the central training institute was provided by this committee. The main objective of such institution was to provide first class coaches or very efficient coaches for different sports and games. Government of India deputed a two member committee of All India Council of Sports, which consisted of Shri M.K. Kaul and Shri M.N. Kapoor. They were being deputed to the Olympic Games, which were held in the year 1960 at Rome. To study the sports institutions and sports organisations, these committee also visited various nations of the world. On the basis of recommendations made by ad-hoc enquiry committee, this committee was being constituted. Kaul Kapoor Committee was the name which was being given to this committee.

Various courses are being offered by this institute. This institute provides the opportunity to do the diploma course in sports coaching at Patiala. One can undergo a certificate course, which has the duration of six week. This course is specifically designed for the physical educators or coaches, with the objective to encourage them to participate in various sports events. Regular courses are also offered by this institute, the aim of which is to give birth to well qualified coaches. One can do master's degree course in sports coaching, with the help of which quality of coaches can be improved.

Important Functions performed by National Institute of Sports

This institute performs various kinds of functions, which are very importance, some of which are as follows—

i. Producing high calibre coaches.

ii. Promotion of the sports throughout the country.

iii. Providing proper coaching based on scientific principles.

iv. Organisation of National Sports Championship for females in the nation.

v. Establishing sports hostel near the regional coaching centres of the institute.

Thus we see that this institute performs various kinds of important functions and today it is known as SAI NS and NIS in various parts of the country.

International Olympic Committee (IOC)

It is a committee which has been set up in order to control the modern Olympic event. It is an international body. During the International Athletic Congress, that was held in the year 1894 at Paris, this committee was being formed. There were total 15 members in the first committee. Baron de Coubertin selected members of this committee himself.

International Olympic Committee has its headquarters in Lausanne. It is a permanent body which is self-elected. Each country where there is a national Olympic committee, will nominate atleast its one member in the committee. The country where once Olympic events have been conducted, have the right to send two of its member in the committee.

International Olympic Committee performs various kinds of functions, some of the very important of them are as follows :—

a. The place where the championships will be organised is being decided by this committee. The right to decide the days on which games will be held also rests with this committee.

b. For conducting the competition and general programmes for the Olympics, fundamental rules and regulations are set-up by this committee.

Programmes of Olympic Spirits and celebration of the Olympic Day or Week are also formulated by this committee, which are being implemented through the National Olympic Committees and various sports organisations.

Programme of Olympic Spirit : This programme is being conducted by the committee to encourage the spirit of Olympic among the young people of the country. It is through this programme that this committee ensures that it do not consider the performance of the players more important, but the social, educational, aesthetic and ethical values which various kinds of sports and games possess.

Indian Olympic Association (IOA)

It was in the year 1927 that Indian Olympic Association came into existence. The honour of becoming its first president was enjoyed by Mr. Dorabji Tata. Since then, this association is functioning very efficiently and is being affiliated with International Olympic Committee.

Once in four years, elections of this association take place. These take place at the annual meeting of the General assembly the purpose being to elect members of the councils. Council consists of various members, like a president, vice presidents which should be nine in numbers, a secretary general, joint secretaries who should be six in number, a treasurer, seven members which should be elected from various representatives of State Olympic Associations and twelve members which should be elected from the representations of National Sports Federation or Associations.

Aims and Objectives of Indian Olympic Association

Indian Olympic association is being set-up with the following objectives :—

a. Development and promotion of the Olympic movement and amateur sports.

b. Enforcement of all rules and regulations of the International Olympic Committee and Indian Olympic Association.

c. Promotion and encouragement of the physical, moral and cultural education of the young people of the nation so that their character can be developed.

d. To be the official organisation in complete forma and whole charge of all the matters relating to Olympic event.

e. Maintenance of highest ideals of amateurism and promotion of interest therein is one of an important objective of Indian Olympic Association. This is kept in mind particularly in relation to Olympic Games.

f. To provide assistance or guidance in cooperation with National Sports Federation in selecting, training and coaching the players of the team. After selecting the players of the team, it is also the function of the association to control and supervise the participants of the team in proper manner.

2

TEACHING METHODS IN PHYSICAL EDUCATION

TEACHING METHODS—MEANING AND SCOPE

Teaching is considered as an art which encompasses not only the good classroom sittings and lengthy and tidy discussion but it is consisted of all those situations in which the educator comes into contact with the students any where across the world. In the field of physical education, a teacher or instructor has to perform multifarious responsibilities viz., he has to teach his pupils some skills; he has to supervises some others; he has to give coaching to the athletes, he has to conduct the competitions and so on; he performs all these activities in order to achieve the higher accomplishments.

All the spheres of education is generally concerned with learning; the process of modification of the behaviour of an individual through experience. Usually an individual learn himself without any help in order to be an acceptable member of the society, this is one of the modes of the human behaviour. While some of the modes of behaviour are to be achieved during one's life time while much of the innate and unlearnt behaviour is to be modified.

The older generation helps the younger generation in the acquisition of new responses and this is the basis of teacher-learning process in the educational institutions. No teaching can be possible without the essence of learning on the part of the disciples or pupils. In other words, we can say that teaching and learning are inter-related and inseparable. Though they are not synonymous yet without one the other is meaningless and worthless.

It is believed by educators that student teaching is one of the most important aspects of the professional preparation of teachers. Those responsible for designing the student-teaching program must remember that the experiences of the student teacher should be a series of activities as nearly like the real teaching situation as possible.

In physical education, the teacher usually adopt a method which decidedly has far reaching effects on the learning of his students due to the complexity of the task involved in the field of physical education which is a wonderful confluence of theory and practice. It is due to defective and inefficient methods and techniques that many a teacher usually failed to deliver the good to his pupils.

Generally, a skilful teacher is easily distinguishable from the one who is unskilled. Moreover, no one can easily learn and apply the skill so easily as it is the result of long years of industry, patience, endurance and experience.

Through many and varied experiences, opportunities should be provided for physical education student teachers to develop the ability:

1. To motivate pupils to develop and maintain good health and physical fitness;

2. To guide learners in the pursuit of knowledge and skills;

3. To prepare boys and girls to become socially competent and worthwhile citizens; and

4. To prepare pupils to assume their responsibilities in a democratic society.

It is generally recognized in the profession that there is great significant in the student-teaching experience as part of teacher preparation. Student teaching is a basic requirement for state certification and a principal prerequisite for the approval of an institution by the National Council for the Accreditation of Teacher Education.

Student teaching is the time when the student tests the knowledge and techniques he has learned in professional courses in the light of their practically, feasibility, and effectiveness in a particular situation.

This is the time that the student teacher puts into practice theories of education, along with his own ideas, so that he becomes skilled, and ready for a full-time teaching position. Since it is a time for the student teacher to practice, some educators refer to this experience as "practice teaching".

In order for the student-teaching experience to be productive and worthwhile, it is essential to have the cooperation of three people:

1. The supervising teacher, who is a regular teacher of physical education in the school and who has been delegated by the school to supervise the student teacher;

2. The college supervisor, who represents the college or university and assigns and prejudicially supervises

student teachers in schools; and

3. The student teacher, the focal point of both the college supervisor and the supervising teacher.

He has a dual responsibility, in that he is a student at the college or university and he is teaching pupils in a school.

For children to reach their full potential in our schools, it would seem to be essential that teachers engage in effective teaching practices. Classroom based investigation has been able to determine effective research-based teaching practices that are related to positive learning outcomes. This understanding has led to the use of the term effective teaching.

The majority of the research on effective teaching has been conducted in the classroom environment, concentrating on more traditional subject areas such as mathematics and language arts. A relatively small amount of information has been gathered in the area of physical education. Consequently, knowledge of what is effective teaching in physical education and how it supports student-learning outcomes is relatively thin, with only a small number of studies providing insight. It is a research gap that needs to be attended to if teachers of physical education are to truly understand how to support student learning by effective teaching.

EFFECTIVE TEACHING

Classroom Research

Although teaching has been a focus of attention for many years, research on teaching is still a relatively new field of inquiry. Initially, studies tended to be focused on teachers, not on the learning environment, trying to identify characteristics or qualities of effective teachers.

For example, the initial idea of an effective teacher in the early 1900s was a judgement primarily based on the "goodness" of a person. Honesty, generosity, friendliness, dedication, and consideration were all regarded to be vital components of an effective teacher. These personal qualities needed to be demonstrated in an authoritarian, disciplined, and organized classroom. Unfortunately, this definition of an effective teacher lacked any objective standards of performance.

It was not until the 1960s that there was a shift in the focus from the personal characteristics of teachers to teacher and student behaviours. For the first time, researchers began to visit classrooms to gather information, specifically to study teacher and student interactions. Instruments were developed to measure classroom interactions: frequency of interaction, types of questions, and response rates. These instruments were employed in research studies in the belief that effective teaching behaviours could be identified and, once identified, could be taught to teachers.

During the 1980s, research tried to identify the facets of classroom teaching that promoted an effective learning environment for children. Much of what we do know about effective teaching comes from this research base. These well-conducted classroom research studies attempted to identify what teachers do to produce student learning.

In a review of research studies that showed an impact on student achievement and learning, Borich summarized effective teaching methods and outlined five key teaching behaviours that were supported by research: lesson clarity; instructional variety; teacher task orientation; engagement in the learning process;

and student success rate. Borich also found that five other behaviours seem to be related to effective teaching. He identified this second group of teaching behaviours as helping behaviours. However, the research identifying these helping behaviours is not as extensive as the research support for the original five key behaviours, and so the findings are not as conclusive. Nevertheless, using student ideas and contributions, structuring, questioning, probing, and teacher affect have been identified as additional behaviours that act as a catalyst to enhance the performance of the five key behaviours.

Research on Teaching in Physical Education

As the majority of the research on effective teaching has been concentrated in traditional academic subject areas such as mathematics and language arts, physical educators were left to develop their own parallel research studies that were specific to their context. Hence, compared to most school subjects, physical education was a late arrival on the teacher effectiveness scene. The major research studies involving effectiveness in physical education have studied such areas as student engagement, curriculum time allocation, teaching methods, teacher behaviour, and teacher perceptions, but have not applied the classroom research findings identified by researchers such as Borich.

With regard to effective teaching in the realm of physical education, studies indicate that 3 many teachers believe they are teaching effectively. This conclusion is based primarily on the teacher's own perception of important teaching criteria: such as explanation, feedback, demonstration, and student enjoyment. According to Siedentop, for the most part, these perceptions could be considered accurate. Teachers do include explanation, feedback, and demonstration in their lessons, and students do enjoy classes. However, it could be suggested, from the definitions of effective teaching provided by Berliner, Brophy, Gage, Harris and Rosenshine, that such teacher perceptions are not accurate measures of effectiveness since student learning is not considered.

It would seem that if student learning is a goal of teaching, then teachers should view student learning as being of prime importance. However, in the area of physical education, there is research evidence to suggest that this is not necessarily the case.

CHARACTERISTICS OF EFFECTIVE PHYSICAL EDUCATION TEACHING

In a review of physical education teaching research, Silverman suggested the following characteristics for the effective teaching of motor skills: the planning for class management and student learning; the anticipation of situations and contingency plans; the awareness of individual student skill differences and use of such information in planning and monitoring; the acquisition of information to plan; the knowledge of, and when to use, a repertoire of teaching styles; the accuracy and focus of explanation and demonstration; the provision for adequate student practice time; the maximization of appropriate student practice and engagement; the minimization of inappropriate student practice and engagement; and the minimization of pupil waiting.

However, Silverman's review has come under criticism by researchers. For example, one of the criticisms from Dodds and Placek was that the "...list also focuses on what teachers do, ignoring both the specific student outcomes that accrue as a result and intended teacher goals relevant to a given teaching situation". Rink also reviewed the research on effective teaching and identified seven distinct teacher characteristics associated with effective instruction in the physical education realm. She identified the following teacher characteristics: the identification of intended outcomes for learning; the planning of learning experiences to accomplish these outcomes; the presentation of tasks in a clear manner; the organization and management of the learning environment; the monitoring of the environment; the development of the lesson content based on student responses; and the evaluation of the effectiveness of instructional/ curricular process.

Mawer in a review of research and viewpoints on effective teaching of physical education, suggested that the following characteristics are indicative of effective teaching: the planning of work effectively; the good presentation of new material; the organization and management of the learning experiences and students; the active involvement of the teacher in teaching students; the provision of a supportive and positive learning environment; the acquisition of a repertoire of teaching styles; and the ability to teach for the facilitation of student understanding of concepts and lesson content.

The characteristics suggested by Silverman, Rink and Mawer bear some similarity to Borich's work. Several factors such as lesson clarity, structure, involving student ideas, and instructional variety have a commonality among the lists. However, there seems to be little, if any, research that has directly looked at the suggested characteristics of effective teachers from the research reviews of Silverman, Mawer, Rink or Borich to determine if the identified characteristics actually do affect student learning in the physical education domain.

The purpose of the present study was to gain an understanding of what is effective teaching in physical education. This is a research gap that needs to be attended to if teachers of physical education are to truly understand how to support student learning. Therefore, this research study examined the effectiveness of a teacher development program on teacher behaviour and, ultimately, the student-learning environment in a physical education setting.

Research Design

The research study utilized two methods of data gathering. A single-case, multiple baseline design was employed to determine the effectiveness of the teacher development program intervention strategy and interviews were conducted in order to understand the teachers' opinions of the teacher development program and their teaching and also to understand the students' opinions of their physical education lessons.

The independent variable in this study was a teacher development program. The program was developed from the conclusions drawn from classroom research and from the opinions of physical education researchers about effective teaching characteristics. The dependent variables in this study were the student behaviours that have been identified by researchers as being important determinants of lesson effectiveness for student learning. These variables were the amount of lesson time that students spent: waiting; in transition; in management activity; in inappropriate activity; receiving information; in engaged activity, and in off-task activity. Student behavioural data were collected through the use of a systematic observation system, Duration Recording. Teacher opinions of the teacher development program were collected through personal interviews. Similarly, student data were also collected through interviews in order to understand their opinions of their physical education lessons.

Participants

Three generalist trained elementary school teachers from the same elementary school were selected for this research study. The selection of the three teachers was based upon their declared personal interest in participating in the research study. All three teachers were female and their years of teaching experience ranged from three to nineteen years. Teacher A was a female, grade 4/5 teacher with 25 students in her class; Teacher B taught a grade 2 class with 22 students, and Teacher C taught 24 students in her grade 1 class. Students were also considered as participants within the research study. Six students from each of the three classes were randomly chosen to provide information concerning their opinions of their physical education lessons.

The Teacher Development Program

Each teacher participated in a teacher development program. The program was introduced to the teachers in the form of a professional development program. A total of 5.5 hours of individual sessions was provided to each teacher. All three teachers received the same topics in the same set order.

Topic #1 - The role of physical education for children. This topic area investigated the role of physical education. In particular, the aims and goals of a quality physical education program were discussed, together with the importance of physical education in the overall educational experience of children. A critical component of this topic was the development of the participant's knowledge and understanding of the value of physical education. Issues such as health and fitness, growth and development, active lifestyle, skill development, personal and social development, self-confidence and self-esteem, and goal setting were addressed in order to for the participant to understand the qualities and the benefits of a quality physical education program. Participants were exposed to research findings that support the inclusion of physical education in the overall educational experiences of children to illustrate the value of physical education in the holistic development of students.

Topic #2 - The importance and understanding of developmental appropriateness. In this topic, information was presented and discussed to enhance an understanding of what developmental appropriateness is in a physical education setting, what constitutes a developmentally appropriate program, and how such a program can be designed by a teacher to meet the developmental needs of the children in his/her class. In particular, the following were covered: (a) what a developmentally appropriate physical education program consists of ; (b) what programs need to be and how they can be taught in order to recognize the unique needs of the individual based on his/her cognitive, emotional and social, and physical needs; (c) what the three developmental levels commonly found in elementary school settings are (Developmental Level I - Kindergarten to Grade 2, Developmental Level II - Grades 3 and 4, Developmental Level III - Grades 5 and 6); (d) what the characteristics are that children at these levels exhibit; (e) what the particular learning requirements children in these levels have, and (f) what teaching considerations are required to support learning opportunities at each developmental level.

Topic #3 - Putting theory into practice. The third topic in the teacher development program considered the issue of taking the theoretical information identified in the review of related literature and placing it into the day-to-day practice of teaching. This topic introduced the research work of Borich and the reviews conducted by Silverman, Rink, and Mawer in order to develop a knowledge of the identified effective teaching behaviours and characteristics of teachers, and how this knowledge can be incorporated into regular teaching practice in physical education lessons. The teacher participants were engaged in discussion about how and why each of the identified teaching characteristics is essential for effective teaching. For example, behaviours such as planning were discussed as it is identified as an effective teaching behaviour.

Topic #4 - Effective teaching. The importance of student learning in physical education was stressed in this topic. The research work of Placek, Schempp, and Hickson and Fishburne were presented and discussed. Ideas for planning for student learning were explored and developed. In particular, the notion of Busy, Happy, and Good was discussed in regard to the issues that make a lesson effective. The effective teaching strategies/ techniques presented in the previous session were considered in regards to personal teaching habits.

Topic #5 - Instructional strategy. This topic aimed to develop an understanding of what a teacher can do to improve his/her instructional strategy. The understanding and selection of teaching styles and methods that are most effective in physical education settings were explored, as was the importance of student engagement, and management of the learning environment. Participants were introduced to the factors that influence the choice of teaching style and method, for example the learning outcome aimed for, the needs of the learner, the lesson content, and the environment. Also, different teaching strategies were considered. For example, the effectiveness of station work when limited equipment is available, the use of task cards to focus student attention and learning and to minimize time students spent receiving instructions.

Topic #6 - The effective teaching model, the theoretical framework, and its implementation. The effective teaching model, designed specifically for this study, was introduced in this topic. The model was developed from the review of related research to provide a focus for the teacher development program. The model incorporated the teacher characteristics that are associated with effective instruction in physical education. The model consisted of three distinct phases: a thought and planning phase, a decision-making and action phase, and a reflection phase. The structure and content of the teaching model is illustrated in Figure 1. The three-phase model was explained and discussed so the participant understood the various components associated with the model and the theoretical framework upon which it is based. The three phases were discussed and attention was drawn to important features. For example in Phase I, the thought and planning phase of the model, the teacher needs to consider two important features: the determination of student needs and the planning for student learning. This requires the teacher to decide upon the needs of the students in the class with regard to the choice of activity, the developmental appropriateness of the activity, and the curricular relevance and when planning for student learning to determine exactly what is the learning outcome for the lesson and how it might best be achieved. It was discussed why this phase would occur prior to the lesson being taught and comparisons were made between the present practice of the teacher participant and what was aimed for.

In Phase II, the decision-making and action phase of the model considers what needs to occur during the lesson. It was explained that the teacher needed to consistently consider and assess what is occurring in the lesson and how it serves the learning needs of the students. Teaching style and method, clarity of presentation, the provision of positive and well-managed environment in order to support and optimize the learning situation, and the need to ensure that there is a high level of student engagement were all brought to the teacher's attention importance discussed. Phase III of the model consists post-lesson reflection and the evaluation of effectiveness. It was discussed with the teacher participants that in this phase, the teacher needed to reflect upon the choices, decisions, and actions made during the first two phases of the model. The teacher also needed to evaluate the lesson content and what student learning occurred. From this reflection and evaluation of the effectiveness of what occurred prior to and during the lesson, decisions could be made for future lesson planning, content, and direction.

Delivery of the Teacher Development Program Intervention Strategy

The teacher development program was provided to the teachers in an individual nature. A multiple-baseline design achieved a time-lagged control through the systematic implementation of the teacher development program intervention. The teacher development program intervention was provided to Class A while maintaining a baseline condition in Classes B and C. The teacher development program intervention was then introduced to Class B while maintaining baseline conditions in Class C. Finally; Class C received the same intervention as Classes A and B.

The multiple-baseline design illustrates the effect of an intervention by demonstrating an accompanying change at the time of the introduction of the intervention strategy. The strength of the design is realized if, following the introduction of the teacher development program intervention, a change is seen in Class A and not in Classes B and C. Consequently, greater strength is realized if corresponding changes occur in Classes B and C after the introduction of the teaching model intervention. This enables any changes to be attributed to the intervention strategy.

The study design involved the observation of three teachers and their physical education classes. Each class was observed for three lessons prior to the commencement of data collection. These lessons allowed for the children in each class to become comfortable with the presence of the researcher and a video camera in the gymnasium. After allowing for an acclimatization period, further lessons were video taped and used for data analysis.

Data Collection

The Duration Recording observation method was used to determine any changes in student behaviours through out the study. Duration recording is a systematic observation instrument that describes how students spend their time. The amount of time that students are involved in behaviours such as receiving instructions, managerial activities, and engaged activity were identified by Siedentop and Tannehill as important for researchers to investigate when studying class environments.

In duration recording, the observer records student behaviour throughout the lesson. Behaviours are recorded according to categories established prior to the onset of data collection. During observation, the observer constantly assesses what 51% of the students in the class are doing. When 51% of the students change what they are doing to another behaviour, the observer makes note of the time, decides on the context of the behaviour and records the behaviour on a recording sheet. Resulting data can be analyzed in terms of the percentage of lesson time spent by the students in each of the established categories. Duration recording can provide a measure of students' opportunities to practice or learn in a class setting. Rink concluded that high levels of activity are desirable and that teachers should aim for an activity time level of at least 50% of the total time of a physical education class. As the instrument also allows for the recording of categories other than activity time, teachers can see where time is being spent that can be changed in order to increase activity time.

To gain insight into the opinions of teachers and students regarding their physical education lesson experiences interview data were collected from the participants. Open format questions were utilized in the personal interview settings. Each of the three teachers involved in the study were interviewed at the onset and at the conclusion the study. Six randomly chosen students from each class were also interviewed in the same manner. The information gained from these interviews provided an understanding of the opinions of the students of their physical education lessons, and the opinions of the teachers concerning the teacher development program and its implementation.

Prior to introducing the teacher development program, teachers were asked to respond to the following style of questions. How would you describe your typical physical education class? What kinds of challenges, if any, are there that you as a teacher of physical education face on a daily or periodic basis? How much time do you normally spend preparing for a typical physical education class? After the teacher development program, the questions focused if changes had occurred. For example, do you think that your teaching has changed? If so, how? What are your opinions of the effective teaching model? Do you think that there has been any change in the students? If so, what? The students were also asked to respond to questions about their physical education lessons. Questions prior to the introduction of the teacher development program were designed to gather information about what had been occurring in their lessons.

Major Findings

The teacher development program attempted to change the teaching behaviour of the three participating teachers and hence impact student behaviour. As Wade suggested, teacher development programs need to not only influence teacher knowledge but also change teacher behaviour and ultimately student learning. Therefore, it was important to intervene upon those variables in the student-learning environment that are controlled by the teacher and that impact the learning environment for students. Namely, the time spent by students in such things as: waiting; transition; management; inappropriate activity; receiving information; engaged activity, and off-task activity.

According to Rink, effective teachers need to minimize the time students spend in activities that are management, transition, inappropriate, or off-task related and maximize the time spent engaged in activity. Minimizing the time spent in non-learning activities and maximizing the amount of time in activities promoting opportunities for learning provides students with optimal learning environments. Rink further suggested that effective teachers needed to attain student activity engagement rates of at least 50% in their lessons.

Prior to the introduction of the teacher development program, student activity engagement rates were not at a level, according to Rink, for optimal student learning to occur. For the three physical education class environments, the mean amount that students were engaged in appropriate activity was 26.5% of lesson time. However, post-intervention results of a mean of 72.0% clearly illustrate that the teacher development program changed the teaching behaviour of the three teacher participants and, hence, provided the students with a far greater amount of engaged activity time.

Consequently, positive changes also occurred in the other variables in the student-learning environment that were controlled by the teacher such as the amount of time that students spent waiting, in transitional activities, in management situations, in inappropriate activity, receiving information, and in off-task activity. For example, a large decrease was evident in the amount of time that students were listening to the teacher. Prior to the implementation of the teacher development program, students spent a mean of 26.5% of lesson time receiving information, after implementation, the time decreased to a mean of 13.8%. Likewise, wait time decreased from a mean of 5.9% to 0.8% of lesson time, student engagement in inappropriate activity decreased from a mean of 4.3% of lesson time to a mean of 0%, transition time decreased from 11.9% to 9.3%, management activities fell from 6.3% to 2.8%, and off-task behaviours decreased from 9.3% to 1.3% of lesson time. These changes, together with the increase in activity-engaged time, provided the students with an environment that was more conducive to learning than it was prior to the introduction of the teacher development program. As the changes coincided with the introduction of the teacher development program, the positive changes in activity engaged time and decreases in the amount of student time associated with ineffective time use could be attributed to the teacher development program.

A second source of data was gained through teacher and student interviews. The teacher participants provided insight regarding the teacher development program and their teaching of physical education lessons, while the students provided information concerning their physical education lessons. Teacher A declared that her understanding of physical education had changed due to the program. She reported feelings of more confidence, had come to appreciate and understand the planning process better, and had begun to plan for student engagement. Teacher A also reported that being part of the teacher development program was rewarding and beneficial to her professional growth and further remarked that she had successfully used the effective teaching model presented to her in the program in other curricular areas of her teaching in order to increase the amount of learning in other subject areas.

Teacher B initially described herself as "...self-taught, not familiar with the curriculum". However, participation in the study caused Teacher B to declare that she had become much more aware of the role of physical education in a child's overall scholastic development. Similar to Teacher A, Teacher B also remarked that her planning for physical education lessons had changed and lessons had begun to focus on on-task behaviours, student learning, and providing students with developmentally appropriate challenges. Teacher B also concluded that her involvement in the teacher development program was worthwhile and beneficial and that her teaching practices had improved. She also stated that she would continue to use the effective teaching model in her physical education teaching and she, too, would also use it in other subject areas as it had "...changed my teaching practice for the better."

Teacher C enjoyed teaching physical education and had, at the start of the study, described herself as having a comfortable level of knowledge with regards to physical education. She had also participated in a number of professional development activities and regarded planning as an important part of the process of teaching physical education. Although there was an initial level of comfort, at the conclusion of the study, Teacher C found that her understanding of physical education had changed due to her participation. She suggested that she had begun to understand the importance of physical education in the overall development of children and now viewed physical education as a core subject. Teacher C further reported that her teaching had changed for the better. It had become more developmentally appropriate and the quality of the instruction that she provided to her students had improved. Teacher C stated that her participation in the teacher development program was extremely beneficial and professionally rewarding.

In regards to the effective teaching model, Teacher C felt that it was very effective and that it had also had an effect on her teaching in other subject areas, "the level of engagement, especially my language arts, math, and science activity centres has increased significantly through using the same model...I also feel that in these subject areas, my instruction is more effective".

Overall, the opinions expressed by all three-teacher participants indicated that participation in the teacher development program had a very positive effect on their physical education teaching and was viewed by all the teacher participants to be very beneficial to their professional growth. Further, the teacher participants remarked that the effective teaching model had become a regular part of their teaching repertoire and was also being utilized throughout the school curriculum. The teacher development program was viewed to be very useful in their professional growth and was valued tremendously.

The interview data collected from the students provided valuable insight into their opinions of their physical education lessons. Data collected at the onset of the study indicated that physical education lessons were fun and had a very similar format: stretching, running laps, an activity, and ending with more stretching. A thread amongst the student responses concerned the cancellation of physical education lessons for such things as assemblies, finishing class work, special projects, and misbehaviour.

At the conclusion of the study, students identified that changes had occurred and that these changes were for the better. "...doing more things", "...rather than talking or listening or sitting", "...busier", "...I get sweaty" were some of the student comments indicating how lessons had changed. Students had begun to recognize that their lessons were not just keeping them busy, they also noted that they were learning, "...cool, new things". The thought of learning as being part of the physical education lesson was not mentioned at the start of the study. Another theme amongst the responses concerned the use of time. Classes had become "far busier", with "less time spent sitting or watching", and more time spent in performance and practice. Lessons were focussed, had a purpose, and experienced little wasted time ultimately providing extra time for practice and skill improvement. Students also stated that there was a difference in the time allocated to physical education. In a clear change from earlier statements, students thought that their lessons had become more frequent and that "everyone went to the gymnasium" to participate in their physical education lessons.

In order to gain an impartial view, the principal of the school provided some overall thoughts. The principal noted that physical education lessons seemed to have "...greater variety in activity, more involvement of students" and that teachers were "planning and matching of activities to student ability levels." According to the principal, these changes had created a "...strong positive improvement in teaching...more focused on the needs for the students. Students seem more involved, and enjoy the classes more...everyone is active and challenging themselves to some skill or task."

Similar to the teacher participants, the principal also felt that the teacher development program had influenced teaching behaviour beyond the gymnasium, "All that participated seem to have transferred the idea of engagement to other subject areas. Teachers look for ways to fill lesson time with challenges and activities that match student needs." The principal also commented upon the design of the teacher development program, "...staff believed it was the key element to putting in to place the growth in their own teaching repertoires. They loved it!"

Supporting the contention that peer coaching creates a conducive environment for the changing of teaching behaviour, the principal further suggested that the "one-on-one coaching ensured that not only did they improve their teaching in physical education but also their teaching in other subject areas." It was further mentioned that:

Too often we receive simple tricks or one-shot ideas without fully understanding the theory behind a change, by providing the theory as well as modelling and coaching, my teachers were able to own the ideas themselves and transfer it to other places and time.

Finally, the principal commented:

One of my teachers is recognized as being in the top one per cent of teachers in the province and she has told me it has been the best experience she has had in 18 years. She has increased her level of student engagement significantly in all areas of her teaching.

Concluding Thoughts

Numerous educational jurisdictions now refer to life-long active living as a goal of their physical education curriculum. In such curricula, it is hoped that physical education can promote a positive attitude toward physical activity and increase participation rates that can offset and reverse the disturbing present trends of inactivity and poor health in children. It is also thought that a well-structured physical education program can enhance and improve the movement proficiency and self-concept of students, thereby promoting the chances for life-long involvement in physical activity and, ultimately, better health.

As the knowledge, skills, and attitude to become a physically educated person are necessary and key components of a physical education program, educators need to teach for this understanding through effective teaching practices. It is, therefore, essential that such effective teaching practices have student learning as a central consideration and basic tenet. Learning has to be foremost in program planning, lesson delivery, and lesson effectiveness reflection. Teachers of physical education have the responsibility to use those characteristics and skills that are effective for student learning. It is only then that students will receive the instruction that they need to gain the associated health benefits from being physical active and to truly become physically educated.

This study indicates that a teacher development program that emphasizes student learning can change student behaviour and help to promote an effective learning environment. The results stress the importance of teachers utilizing techniques of effective teaching. The three teachers and the learning environment in their physical education lessons experienced positive changes through the application of effective teaching behaviours emphasized in the teacher development program and the effective teaching model. It is recommended that the nature of this study is an important area of future investigation and worthy of further research in order to extend the understanding of effective physical education teaching. Such replication would provide confirmation to the extent that the teacher development program and the effective teaching model are important and valid additions to the physical education teaching literature.

COMMON TERMS USED IN SCHOOL TEACHING

Although there are no standard terms in the vocabulary for student teaching, the following terms are generally accepted by educators:

College supervisor. A member of the college faculty who has the responsibility for supervising student teachers in cooperation with the supervising teacher in the cooperating school.

2. Student teacher. A college student who has completed the minimum requirements for student teaching and has been assigned to a cooperating school for his professional laboratory experiences.

3. Supervising teacher. Sometimes referred to as a cooperating teacher or master teacher in the cooperating school to whom the student teacher is assigned.

4. Cooperating school. An off-campus school which has appropriate facilities and professional for professional laboratory experiences, including student teaching.

5. Student teaching. A period of time when the

student teacher, under the guidance of the supervising teacher and college supervisor; teachers pupils in a cooperating school.

6. Professional laboratory experience. All of the school and community activities of the student teacher which involve observation, participation, teaching, and other leadership opportunities leading to a greater understanding of the teacher's role.

PURPOSES

The major purposes of student teaching are to provide:

1. Direct opportunities of a varied nature which permit first-hand experiences with pupils;

2. Opportunities for the student teacher to put into practice many of the theories studied in various professional preparation courses;

3. A teaching situation involving problems which the future teacher has an opportunity to analyse; and

4. Situations where teaching skills and competencies are developed.

The objectives of student teaching in physical education, in particular, are as follows:

1. To provide experiences which will develop the student teacher's ability to teach skills and knowledge in a variety of activities.

2. To provide experiences in which the student teacher learns to evaluate pupils in terms of physical fitness, skills, knowledge, and social competence.

3. To provide experiences in which the student teacher will work with pupils in many school situations, including the gymnasium, swimming pool, athletic field,

and playground.

4. To provide experience which will lead the student teacher to recognize, adjust to, and make provisions for individual differences in the skills of pupils.

5. To provide experiences which will enable the student teacher to view the school as a whole and to learn his responsibility in carrying out administrative policies and in accomplishing the general objectives of the school program.

6. To provide experiences which will stimulate the student teacher's desire for continuous professional and academic growth.

7. To help the student teacher to use the needs, problems, and interests of the pupils as a basis for planning, developing, and evaluating their learning experiences.

8. To provide experiences that will give the student teacher the opportunity to work with parents, teachers, and others in promoting physical education.

9. To provide experiences in which the student teacher learns to develop the ability to handle daily class routine.

10. To provide experiences which will give the student teacher an opportunity to work with pupils of all ages.

11. To help the student teacher discover, use, and appraise groups processes that promote effective human relations.

12. To provide experiences that will give the student teacher the opportunity to plan units of work and to

make daily lesson plans.

13. To provide experiences in which the student teacher has the opportunity to use many techniques of instruction and to develop his teaching skills to the point where he is competent to handle many teaching situations independently.

14. To provide experiences that will enable the student teacher to develop into a well-balanced individual, a person possessing a pleasing personality and desirable personal characteristics.

15. To provide experiences in which the student teacher establishes learning situations designed to develop critical thinking on the part of pupils.

16. To provide the student teacher with opportunities for self-analysis and for the development of self-confidence.

17. To provide experiences in which the student teacher learns to select, use, and interpret objectives data and records so as to understand and guide the pupil's growth.

18. To provide experiences which create an understanding of human development both physical and mental.

19. To provide experiences which will enable the student teacher to learn how the school and community can work together.

20. To provide experiences which will enable the student teacher to become familiar with professional literature, textbooks, reference materials, community resources, and teaching equipment, particularly in physical education.

21. To establish within the student teacher the feeling that he belongs to the school and has responsibilities equal to that of a full-time teacher.

GETTING TO KNOW THE SCHOOL AND COMMUNITY

It is very important that the student teacher become acquainted with the community in which he will reside and the school in which he will teach, of he is to become an effective member of the teaching staff.

By studying the people in the local situation very carefully he can learn things which may directly affect the pupil-teacher relationship in the physical education program.

It is also important that the supervising teacher create opportunities, not only in the teaching station but also in the school and community, for the student teacher to participate in school and community affairs.

Often, this requires special planning because special arrangements have to be made. The supervising teacher has the responsibility for seeing that the student teacher has varied and extensive experiences outside of his regular teaching.

By participating in the total school program, the student teacher:

a. Can gain greater insight into the problems and complexities of the day-to-day operation of today's schools.

b. Will meet and get to understand the problems of other school personnel, such as principles, guidance counsellors, and custodians, as they relate to the total school program including physical education.

c. Will have an opportunity to display a particular

talent or skill he may possess.

d. Will have an opportunity to meet every teacher in the school on a personnel as well as a professional basis.

e. Can meet with other teachers to observe and analyse different methods, techniques, and philosophies in other areas of education.

f. Will become better acquainted with the pupils and other pupils outside of physical education.

g. Can develop his own social growth by being diplomatic, a good listener, and capable of expressing one's self.

Many of the values of participation in the total school program can also be attained by participation in community affairs.

The student teacher who takes an active part in community activities will develop skills of a personal, social, and professional nature. However, there are certain broader benefits to be achieved, including:

1. The opportunity to meet some of the parents of the children in his physical education classes.

2. The opportunity for interpreting the physical education program of the school to the community leaders.

3. The opportunity for the student teacher to be accepted and to gain respect in the community.

4. The opportunity to see what part community leaders have in determining school policies.

5. The opportunity to observe his pupils interact with their parents and other adults in situations outside of the school, which should give the student teacher a better

understanding of his pupils.

6. The opportunity to meet some of the leaders of the community.

7. The opportunity to discuss the needs of the physical education program with members of the community.

WHAT MAKES A GOOD STUDENT TEACHER

It is generally agreed that a good physical education student teacher is distinguished by:

1. Initiative, interest, and enthusiasm in solving problems.

2. A professional and mature attitude toward his work and his colleagues.

3. Acceptable standards of cleanliness and neatness.

4. A sincere interest in teaching as a career.

5. Willingness to read professional literature in physical education and in general education.

6. His appreciations of the chance to learn and improve his essential skills in teaching physical education.

7. Behaviour that is acceptable in his school and community.

8. An attitude of inquiry toward everyday situations.

9. A desire to attend and participate in school and community meetings.

10. Thorough preparation and planning for daily teaching responsibilities, including coaching.

3

THE MAINSTREAMED PROGRAMME IN PHYSICAL EDUCATION AND SPORTS

INTRODUCTION

Some impaired children who have special needs are able to succeed in mainstreamed or regular physical education classes. They are allowed to remain as long as they can "meet the challenge, " which denotes sufficient skill, strength, and emotional and mental abilities to participate with regular pupils in most of the games, sports, and other activities routinely assigned. "Meeting the challenge" thus suggests the student's ability to cope—to deal with and to overcome at least some problems and difficulties. It does not, however, imply an ability to maintain a contest or meet a challenge on even terms of success.

OBJECTIVES

Realistic set of objectives takes three different instructional areas into account—the program itself, the instructor, and the pupil. Each teacher is responsible for asking, "Is the regular or mainstreamed program right for this particular handicapped child?" Approaching the problem from the other direction, the teacher should ask, "Is this child right for the program?" Most difficult of all to answer is the question, "Am I, as a teacher, knowledgeable and devoted enough to help youngsters at least part of the way toward the programs's stated objectives?" To this end, teachers should, first of all, familiarize themselves with concepts and terms pertaining to students who are impaired. Second, they should seek actual experience with the nature and needs of the impaired. Third, they should ask themselves whether, by temperament or background, they can work with youngsters who are different from the "regular" class members. After analysis of test data a teacher should be ready to define and develop program objectives. Mainstreamed program objectives fall into four major categories:

Physical and Motor Fitness

The development of:

a. Gross motor skills and movements.

b. Physical fitness values.

c. Game and sport skills.

d. Neuromuscular and kinesthetic awareness.

e. Confidence and competence in performing activities.

f. Rhythm, poise, grace, coordination, balance, and reaction time.

Social Adjustment

An appreciation of :

a. Social interactions in a group situation.

b. Acceptable personality traits of others.

c. Socially acceptable emotion and tension outlets.

d. A positive social identify.

e. Achievement and success in oneself and others.

f. Aesthetic and creative values.

Emotional Adjustment

An appreciation of:

a. The benefits of emotional maturity.

b. The right personal attitude toward others.

c. Leisure time as a means of emotional stability.

d. One's body-image and self-concept.

Cognitive Skills

An understanding of:

a. Rules, strategies, and the knowledge of games and sport.

b. The physiological effects of exercise upon the body.

c. Basic body mechanics of human movement.

GUIDELINES FOR PROGRAMMING

Guidelines for the mainstreamed or regular physical education programs include placement, grouping, curriculum, and motivation. With reference to placement, one should distinguish between those students with special physical and motor needs and those who need only accommodations. It is well to avoid uniformity whenever it ignores individual needs. When youngsters with special physical and motor needs are mainstreamed, instructors should avoid having to slow down the others. In grouping, the teacher should avoid holding back the entire class for the benefit of one or two handicapped members.

Instructors should weight the pros and cons of the

competitive sports. Although competitive sports usually accelerate development, they often ignore the individual's interests and abilities. Students should demonstrate ability to perform sequences of related movement before attempting complex activities. The teacher should observe their skills in both locomotor and nonlocomotor movements and judge their performance as individuals, as couples, and as members of a team. In developing the mainstreamed curriculum, the teacher should consider chronological ages since older pupils differ from younger pupils in their physical and social needs.

It is important to bear in mind that neither the rules of a game, nor the style and pace of play are carve in stone. "Flexibility" and "fun" should be watchwords to remember. Activities should be selected that appeal to the personal, social, emotional, and physical interests of students. Good programming calls for instructors to be creative enough to challenge outdated ideas; to know about community resources that might vary and enrich the program; to develop a repertory of alternatives when the weather dictates that classes be held indoors; and to secure additional education on integrating the impaired in the mainstreamed class through conferences, workshops, and in-service training. Guidelines for motivation include giving impaired children a voice in the process of determining ways in which adaptations and accommodations can be made and providing impaired students positive role-models on which to pattern their movements and behaviour. Abilities, not disabilities should be emphasized, by selecting activities that bring success and avoid failure.

CLASS SIZE AND COMPOSITION

While handicapped students are being assimilated into a regular physical activity class, no ready-made formula dictates the cutoff point. Each class has its unique problems. However, a ratio of six to eight non-impaired students to each impaired student in a class of 20 to 25 is possible. If the result is unmanageable, the number of impaired should be reduced. Mental age, chronological age, motor ability, cognitive skill, and both social and emotional stability all figure in decisions on class size and placement; on-the-scene observations are also helpful. Mainstreaming may not run smoothly from the start.

An instructor should be prepared for some rough going in the first meetings of any mainstreamed class. Glaring differences between the "regulars" and the "impaired," obvious discrepancies between the handicapped child's reported potential and what the teacher actually sees, may be frustrating. Fortunately, steps can be taken to soften the blow. The more experienced teachers of mainstreamed classes say that the early briefing sessions with regular students in advance of the arrival of their impaired classmates is highly effective. It is here that instructors can present the problem as an educational opportunity, thus allaying any doubts that linger in young minds about the philosophy, methods, and objectives of the federal mandate. Frankness from the start will hurt no one. Statements that are direct, brief, unsentimental, and free from moralizing work best. The benefits of mainstreaming to the average boy or girl will be born out when time is spent in physical activities with the impaired. School children across the nation are beginning to see that mainstreaming can work—a realization that in itself has immeasurable educational value.

SAFETY MEASURES

The elimination of hazards in facilities, equipment, and procedures is important; but instructors should also regularly question their own procedures and constantly point out hazards to their pupils. The following safety measures to be taken at the planning stage should be applied to facilities, equipment, procedures, and instruction:

1. Has the equipment been safety-checked at each session?

2. Is the program adequately housed? Do gyms and classrooms have ample space for all participants?

3. Have activities been selected that are suitable for performance in the available area?

4. Are play areas cleared of hazards? Has sufficient space been provided outside the boundaries?

5. Have all damaged or defective items of equipment been repaired or placed out of reach?

6. Do the activities match the potential functioning levels of everyone in the mainstreamed class?

7. Have specific safety rules been established and conspicuously displayed?

8. Are children prohibited from performing on equipment that they are not sure how to use?

9. Are teachers competent in administering first aid?

10. Are instructors prepared for accidents at any

time during the activity period?

11. Are eyeglass protectors provided for pupils who need them? These may be worn when playing basketball, softball, volleyball, and floor hockey. Do pupils with contact lenses understand their care and attention?

12. Is the correct and safe use of all gym equipment grasped by everyone in the mainstreamed class?

13. Have students been warned about unnecessary roughness?

14. Does the instructor know how and when to spot fatigue?

The legal responsibilities of an instructor or recreator acting in place of a parent are subject to various interpretations by the courts. To be brief, the law regards as reasonable and prudent those who "anticipate danger and accidents." Therefore, negligence must be determined as the direct cause of an injury before legal proceedings can be started. When a teacher acts negligently, he or she may be sued for damages.

FACILITIES

Adequate space is needed for mainstreaming that meets both quantitative and qualitative specifications. Outdoor facilities for a typical elementary school should have a minimum of five acres of ground plus one additional are for every one hundred pupils. This means that in a 500-pupils school there should be at least ten acres of land. Playground surfaces range from all-weather, safety matting to grass and wood chips for certain sections. Ground should be relatively smooth, well drained, and well landscaped. It should be obvious that surfaces are of critical importance in accident prevention, especially for pupils whose coordination and reflexes are below par. Nor should planners ignore the function of circles and lines when organizing classes. Painted on hardtop surfaces or on safety matting, such boundaries are surprisingly effective. If the outdoor area is near a street, adequate fencing is mandatory. Frequent inspection of playground areas for litter, hard objects, and slip perky surfaces is one way to avoid charges of negligence. At the elementary school level, indoor facilities should include a gymnasium or a large multipurpose room; a swimming pool, indoor or outdoor, obviously enhances any program. Since few school systems can boast all of these, most instructors must learn to improvise.

In addition, the facility should include dressing rooms, shower and drying rooms, team rooms, storage rooms, training room, and offices. A swimming pool is a welcome addition to any mainstreamed program. It should be a requirement in any school physical plant. The accessibility of a gymnasium, pool, or multipurpose room is based on a number of criteria: Are toilets in the gymnasium locker rooms designed to accommodate wheelchairs? Are the was basins, mirrors, towel racks, and drinking fountains at the proper height to accommodate those in wheelchairs? Has at least one shower been designed for wheelchair students? Are the aisles in the locker room wide enough for the free movement of wheelchairs? Are the floors of all locker rooms of the nonskid type?

Are they safe for pupils on crutches as well as for those with braces? Is the traffic patterns controlled throughout the facility? Are corridors sufficiently wide to accommodate the impaired? Are signs and markings either in Braille or in raise letters? Are audio-cassettes or other sound-warnings available to assist the blind?

Have lights or alternative signals and warnings been installed for the hearing-impaired? Do regulation ramps lead into the pool building and into the water at poolside? Is there a lift in the pool? Although architectural barriers cannot always be eliminated without great expense, school boards should be alerted to all structural deficiencies and make arrangements to correct them.

4

RESEARCH PROGRAMS AND METHODS IN PHYSICAL EDUCATION

As a part of teaching profession, physical education has long been recognized, evidenced by its affiliation with the National Education Association since 1937. Even earlier, in 1885, a group of teachers and other interested individuals formed the Association for the Advancement of Physical Education to encourage the exchange of program and instructional ideas. The American Alliance for Health, Physical Education, Recreation and Dance today, along with a multiplicity of affiliated organizations, promotes physical education, sports, leisure, and fitness.

PHYSICAL EDUCATION AS A PROFESSION

We need to define a profession before looking specifically at physical education. A profession requires extensive period of training, has an intellectual component that must be mastered, offers opportunities for communication among its members, and provides an important service that is recognized by society. Physical educators usually have at least a bachelor's degree and frequently have advanced study and training in an extensive body of knowledge that takes considerable time and effort to learn. Colleagues in related careers share research findings and new ideas while serving people in all aspects of society. The following overview of the structure and activities of the American Alliance demonstrates that physical education qualifies as a profession.

NATIONAL ESTABLISHMENT AND SERVICES

The American Alliance for Health, Physical Education, Recreation and Dance (AAHPERD, or the Alliance) has enjoyed a century of service and growth (from 49 to more than 37,000 members). According to Executive Vice President Jack Razor, No other organization in America can match the scope of our efforts and the impact we are having.

We can be proud of all that we do. The breadth of our services and the many lives that we touch indirectly and directly serve together as an essential catalyst for our continuing viability and a foundation upon which to build. One reason for the widespread influence of the AAHPERD is the many professional groups that have merged into its structure. In 1937, as a department of the National Education Association, the former American Physical Education Association became the American Association for Health and Physical Education. (It became an alliance in 1974.) Recreation was added to its title in 1938, and dance was added in 1979.

The Alliance's missions are to improve the quality of school programs and to enhance positive life-style changes for all Americans. It is headquartered in Reston, Virginia. Its objectives are follows (AAHPERD By-laws):

1. Professional growth and development— to support, encourage, and provide guidance in the development and conduct of programs in health,

leisure, and movement-related activities which are based on the needs, interests, and inherent capacities of the individual in today's society;

2. Communication— to facilitate public and professional understanding and appreciation of the importance and value of health, leisure, and movement-related activities as they contribute toward human well-being;
3. Research—to encourage and facilitate research which will enrich the depth and scope of health, leisure and movement-related activities; and to disseminate the findings to the profession and other interested and concerned publics;
4. Standards and guidelines—to further the continuous development and evaluation of standards within the profession for personnel and program in health, leisure, and movement-related activities;
5. Public affairs— to coordinate and administer a planned program of professional, public, and governmental relations that will improve education in area of health, leisure, and movement-related activities.

The services provided by the Alliance are also varied. For example, in 1958 the Alliance developed the Youth Fitness Test, the first of its kind with national norms and fitness standards for boys and girl aged 10 to 17 years. In 1980, the Alliance launched its Health Related Physical Fitness Test, which measures cardiorespiratory function, body composition, strength, and flexibility.

Other services include holding an annual convention; publishing brochures, research abstracts, books, conference proceedings, and other information pertinent to its fields of interest; positively influencing public opinion and leg- isolation; and providing consultant services. Three periodicals are published by the Alliance. The *Journal of Physical Education, Recreation and Dance* includes articles of a broad and practical nature, while the *Research Quarterly for Exercise and Sports* reports research findings. Update, in newspaper format, keeps the membership apprised of current events and legislation.

The following discussion describes the six associations that constitute the Alliance.

The American Association for Leisure and Recreation promotes leisure services at the local and national levels and recreation education in the schools. Areas of concern and services include leisure education in higher education, the place of recreation in American society, continuing education workshops, bicycle education, and legislative support for outdoor recreation resources. Programs of health education in school, communities and colleges are the purview of the Association for the Advancement of Health Education Health issues are vigorously promoted by this association through position papers; leadership for projects such as the drinking/driving problem is provided; and health education legislation is actively supported.

The Association for Research, Administration, Professional Councils and societies is composed of 10 special-interest groups, including the Aquatics Council, the College and University Administrators Council, the Council of city and county Directors, the council on Outdoor Education, the Therapeutics Council, the Council on Facilities and Equipment, the International

Relations Council, the Measurement and Evaluation Council, and the Physical Fitness Council. Among the varied professional services these groups provide is co-sponsorship of the FITNESSGRAM with the President's Council on Physical Fitness and sports, the Institute for Aerobics Research and the Campbell Soup Company. The project provides parents with a computerized fitness report card of their child's test results on the AAHPERD Youth Fitness Test or on the Health Related Physical Fitness Test.

The student Action Council, the tenth special-interest group, has served student members of the Alliance and has worked with collegiate majors' clubs since 1969. Because the future of the profession and its organization depends on today's student, it is essential that student become actively involved in professional activities. The objectives of the student Action Council include improving local, state, district, and national student programs, providing opportunities for student leadership experiences, supporting and promoting youth service projects, and serving as an advocate for maximum involvement of student on all Alliance associations. This group also promotes the active involvement of student in local physical education majors' clubs as avenues for leadership and enhanced professional preparation. The National for girls and Women is sport seeks to improve and to expand sport opportunities for girls and women at all levels of competition. One major effort has been the training of officials through its Affiliated Boards of Official.

The National Association for Girls and Women in Sports and the National Association for Sports and Physical Education share leadership in the National Council of Athletic Training and the National Intramural

Sports Council. The largest of the Alliance associations, the National Association for Sports and Physical Education, Promotes physical education and sports for all people through its numerous substructures and activities. Its Physical Education Justification Packet helps colleagues whose programs are threatened by economic cutbacks and lack of community support by providing materials such as documented research survey results and statements relative to the importance of physical education in the daily lives of students. Physical Education Public Information (PEPI) actively spreads the word about physical education through print ads, pamphlets, public service announcements, and the observance of the annual National Physical Education and sport Week. Ten academies (Adapted Physical Education, Curriculum, Exercise Physiology, History, Kinesiology, motor Development, philosophy, psychology, sociology, and sport Art) play an integral role in enhancing research. Five special-interest council are also a part of the National Association for sport and Physical Education; these are the council on Physical Education for Children, the Secondary School Physical Education Council, the college and University Physical Education Council, the College and University Physical Education Department Administrators Council, and the National Council of Secondary Athletic Directors.

The National Dance Association, the only association serving dance as education, promotes dance through conferences, workshops, publications, research, and realisations with numerous groups, such as the Kennedy Centre for the performing Arts' education program and the National Endowment for the Arts. It cooperates with Dance USA to promote National Dance Week.

The Alliance is divided into six district associations that share the goals and activities of the Alliance while providing leadership opportunities and services within each region. Memberships in the Alliance and in a district are combined, thus enabling professionals to attend their district's and the Alliance's annual conventions. Non-convention workshops, clinics, seminars, and other learning opportunities provide Alliance members with the latest research findings, innovative activities, and teaching approaches and provide opportunities for personal enrichment and growth. Most state associations, state departments of education, and other physical education-related organizations also provide year-round programming.

Each state also provides professional the opportunity to learn different coaching techniques, to acquire new skills, and to interact and exchange information with other members at its annual convention. Students especially you, should take advantage of state conventions, because not only will you learn from these experiences, but you also may make contact with many individuals who later may hire you or help you to get a job. The aims of Physical Education and Recreation like those of other state organization, are consistent with the purposes of general education and relate specifically to the areas of athletics, dance, health education, intramural programs, physical education, and recreation.

These aims include the following :

1. To awaken and stimulate wide and intelligent interest in its areas of concern;
2. To acquire and disseminate accurate professional information.

3. To promote adequate programs in the areas of concern and to advance the standards of teaching and performance in these areas;
4. To cooperate with the Alliance for Health, Physical Education Recreation and Dance, the Southern District Association for Health, Physical Education and Recreation, and other state and national education associations interested in the growth and development of children and adults.

Physical education provides enrichment opportunities to its members as they prepare themselves to serve other. They are joined in their efforts by related groups who seek to share knowledge for the benefit of all.

AFFILIATED ORGANIZATIONS

While the AAHPERD is largest organization associated with physical education and its related fields, it shares its interests with numerous other groups. The discussion that follows briefly describes some of these organizations.

HIGHER EDUCATION

In 1978, the National Association for Physical Education in Higher Education (NAPEHE) was formed by a merger of National Association for Physical Education of College Women and the National College Physical Education Association for Men. Since the merger, NAPEHE has continued the publication of *Quest* and its conference proceedings. Since 1930 the American Academy of Physical Education has been the highest honorary group in health, physical education, and recreation. Its more than 100 members have contributed scholarship and professional service, especially in colleges and universities. Some of their research studies are published annually in *The Academy Papers*. Illustrative of its leadership the Academy, in 1981, identified the following contemporary social problems of import to the professional: that physical educators need to help their clientele in all sectors to discriminate between fact and myth in the developing of fitness, diets, exercise equipment, and health programs; that if moral and ethical values are to result from physical education and athletic programs, teachers and coaches must emphasize them; and that physical educators should share their knowledge with other involved in sport programs for youths to help ensure quality experiences.

HEALTH

Since 1926, the American School Health Association has sought to improve health instruction, healthful living, and health services in the school. Although originally only for physicians, membership is now open to anyone engaged in school health work. This association publishes the *Journal of School Health.*

RECREATION

Development and expansion of programs and services along with environmental concerns constitute the primary work of the National Recreation and Park Association. It is also dedicated to having trained personnel conduct community recreation programs. *The Journal of Leisure Research* and *Parks and Recreation* are its publications. The National Intramural-Recreational Sports Association was begun in 1950 to provide an opportunity for college intramural directors to meet annually to exchange ideas and information. With the expansion of college programs into recreational services of all kinds, the Association assumed its present name in 1975. Sharing innovative program ideas, reporting research, and discussing policy and procedures highlight its annual convention and the *NIRSA Journal.*

SPORTS MEDICINE

The need to establish professional standards and to disseminate information led to the establishment of the National Athletic Trainers' Association in 1950, which publishes *Athletic Training* for its membership. The American College of Sports Medicine was founded in 1954 by individuals drawn from medicine, physiology, and physical education. Among its objectives are advancing scientific studies dealing with the effects of physical activities in health and well-being; encouraging cooperation and professional exchange among physicians, scientists and educators; initiating promoting, and correlating research in sports medicine; and maintaining a sports medicine library. It encourages research publications in injury prevention and rehabilitation and in environmental effects of exercise, nutrition, and other factors through its *Medicine and Science in Sports and Exercise.*

PSYCHOLOGY, HISTORY, PHILOSOPHY, ANTHROPOLOGY, AND SOCIOLOGY

North American Society was founded by the psychologists, psychiatrists, and physical educators for the Psychology of Sport and Physical Activity in 1965 to promote this increasingly popular field of study. Since 1973, the North American Society for Sport History has encouraged scholarly research in all aspects of this discipline of sport, conducted an annual conference, and published the *Journal of Sport History.* The Philosophic society for the Study of sport, founded in

1972, encourages scholarly investigation of the philosophical aspects of sport through its *Journal of the Philosophy of Sport.* Other specialized association are the Association for the Anthropological Study of Play, the North American Society for the Sociology of sport, and the Association for the Advancement of Applied Sport Psychology.

FITNESS

Since 1974, the Association for Fitness in Business has led in the expansion of employee fitness programs through its approximately 2000 members. These exercise-testing technicians, exercise physiologists, recreation specialists, and program directors conduct exercise testing prescribe exercise programs, promote healthful lifestyle changes, and administer programs for corporate executives and employees.

ATHLETICS

In the realm of college athletics, the regulatory bodies include the National Collegiate Athletic Association (founded in 1906), the National Association of Intercollegiate Athletics (founded in 1952), and the National Junior college Athletic Association (founded in 1938). The National Collegiate Athletic Association, with 644 members, promotes competition through 22 championship in 12 sports for women and 42 championships in 19 sports for men. The 520 members of the National Association of Intercollegiate Athletics represent smaller institutions and provided 15 women's and 17 men's championships. The National Junior College Athletic Association conducts championships in 9 sports for women and 12 sports for men.

Other athletic organization that encourage the

exchange of ideas include the college sports Information Directors of American, the College Athletics Business Manager, the National Association of Collegiate Directors of Athletics, and the National strength and Conditioning Association. The Amateur Athletic Union (AAU) was founded in 1888 to promote amateur sports and to check the spread of the problems associated with professional sports. Using more than 300,000 volunteers at the local, regional and national levels, this organization conducts sports events for competitors of all ages. The National Federation of State High School Associations (founded in 1920) and the 50 state high school athletic and/or activities associations work to protect the activity and athletic interests of high school, to promote the growth of educational interscholastic athletics, and to protect high school students from exploitation.

Many state also have coaches' associations that either are specific to one sport or have coaches from all sports in their memberships. These groups usually sponsor statewide or regional workshops or clinics about specific coaching techniques or strategies, rule changes, value and ethics in school athletics, and sport psychology.

YMCA—YWCA

The Young Men's Christian Association, since 1851, and the Young Women's Christian Association, since 1866, have promoted physical activities and sports as will as the development of values. Today, both groups offer a wide range of fitness and sports activities that target all skill and age levels. The basic objectives for all professional groups are to exchange information to learn, and to serve.

To enhance both you knowledge about and

commitment to your chosen career, you should seek opportunities through these organization to grow professionally. By exchanging program ideas and instructional and motivational techniques, members can improve their abilities to serve others and to learn how to communicate their goals and activities to colleagues and to the general pupils. Through the sharing of experience and research, many ideas for further study are generated. Therefore, as a young professional, you are encouraged to join your college, state, and national associations and one or more of those in your interest area. You also should being to read physical education periodicals, as listed in to help you more fully understand your profession.

PROFESSIONAL PREPARATION FOR PHYSICAL EDUCATION PROGRAMS

Assuming that you are considering physical education as a career, the second section of this chapter introduces you to the various tracks or majors that exist in many colleges and universities. This will prepare you for chapter 5, which describes many careers related to physical education, and chapter 6, which explains many specific programs and certifications. Professional preparation programs in physical education traditionally have been oriented toward teacher education with a secondary track or option sometimes available for those interested in physical education in other settings.

Until demand for teachers decreased dramatically in the late 1970s most students completed the first option in case they ever wanted to teach. Seldom dose this occur today due to a surplus of teachers. The tight job market, however, is only one factor in this change. Colleges and universities, in response to the decreasing number of teaching positions, have revised their curricula to include non-traditional tracks. Simultaneously, the popularity of and resultant expansion in fitness, leisure, recreation, athletic, and sports-related activities have created a boom in diversity and availability of careers. Since qualified individuals are needed for these positions, several non-traditional tracks offer specialized course work, internship, and certifications.

TEACHING TRACK

Teacher certification following graduation from an accredited 4-year institution is the goal of the teaching track. This preparation may occur throughout the undergraduate years or may by concentrated in just 2 years or may be concentrated in just 2 years following the completion of general course work taken at a junior or community college or at a 4-year institution. Certification that can be obtained include those of physical education for kindergarten (K) through grade 6; grades 7 through 12; K through 12; health education ; and dance. The National Council for Accreditation of Teacher Education (NCATE) NOW ALLOWS "learned societies" such as the American Alliance for Health Physical Education, Recreation and Dance, to recommend guidelines for the professional studies component of its standards.

These guidelines, containing all the attitudes, knowledge, and skill required of a physical education teacher have been subdivided into three elements: academic, professional and pedagogical. Aquatics, dance exercise, games, sports, and other leisure pursuits are components of the unique academic content of physical education. The applied sciences of motor development, sport management, sport pedagogy, motor learning, sport philosophy, sport biomechanics, adapted physical education, exercise physiology, sport psychology, spot sociology, and the humanities of art, literature, and music, as discussed earlier, provide the intellectual and theoretical base for studies in physical education aspect of the undergraduate program develops an awareness of and commitment to the various educational, research, and service activities of physical education. These include studies in curriculum models, organization structures, diagnostic and evaluative procedures, and problem solving. Knowledge about the teaching and learning of physical skills constitute the pedagogical element. Abilities to plan, implement and evaluate learning are observed in a supervised student teaching experience.

According to the Council on Physical Education for Children, the curriculum for prospective elementary physical educators should develop competence in:

1. Understanding child growth and development, with an emphasis on motor development;
2. A knowledge of and appreciation for the structure and function of human movement;
3. Observing and assessing children and their movement;
4. A knowledge of learning processes, teaching strategies, and factors that affect motor learning;
5. Developing curriculum with emphasis on curriculum designs and strategies appropriate for elementary school programs;
6. Assessing and working with children who have special needs;

7. Personal skills and teaching skills in the content areas of fundamental movement patterns, games/ sports, dance, gymnastics, and aquatics to meet the needs and interests of children in kindergarten through grade six.

Following completion of a program that includes learning and developing these competencies and a supervised student teaching experience in grades K through 6 student receive their certification. Similarly, all prospective work in academic, professional, and pedagogical areas, although specific requirements very by state as they do for elementary school certification.

Students often must complete fieldwork experiences, such as class observations, beginning as early as the first year in college in some programs. These are often used to help student decide whether they wish to pursue a teaching track.

A part of this commitment of teachers at all levels is the belief in and advocacy of the essentiality of physical education in the school. Health education and dance majors have similar requirements, but their academic bodies of knowledge differ from those of the physical education student.

NON-TRADITIONAL TRACKS

Non-traditional tracks or course work options very widely in colleges and universities as each seeks to meet the interests of its student. Six of the most common curricula are listed below.

ATHLETIC TRAINING

Athletic training is currently offered as a undergraduate major in 63 colleges and universities. The curriculum specifies 11 courses emphasizing the sciences and at least 800 hours of clinical experiences for completion.

SPORT OR EXERCISE SCIENCE

A sport or exercise sciences option focuses on courses in chemistry, biology or zoology, anatomy, physiology, biomechanics, and exercise physiology.

This background prepares graduates for advanced studies in one of these scientific fields as well as for careers in which understanding the scientific bases of exercise and sport is vital.

COACHING AND TRAINING

Coaching emphasis or certification program are becoming increasingly popular as junior and senior high school and youth sport leagues want individuals who are trained specifically to work with this population.

The need for coaches of interscholastic teams exceeds the supply due to increased numbers of girls' teams, the hiring of fewer new teachers, and the resignation of tenures physical educator from coaching but not from teaching.

Coaching curricula most often include first aid and care and prevention of athletic injuries, anatomy, physiology, coaching theory and techniques, human growth and development, sport administration or management, sport psychology, and sport pedagogy.

HEALTH AND FITNESS OR FITNESS SPECIALIST

A health and fitness or fitness specialist track combines a scientific foundation, such as in biomechanics and exercise physiology, with business and management courses for physical education-related careers in the public and private sectors. In this option, some emphasis is placed on the teaching of various physical activities.

SPORT COMMUNICATION OR MANAGEMENT

Sport communication seeks to merge knowledge in physical education and sport with skills in English, speech, journalism, and broadcasting. Similarly, sport management combines business and management course work with selected physical education courses. A diversity of courses selected to meet each individual's interests and needs, combined with independent studies emphasizing practical application of knowledge, is the best preparation for careers in these two fields.

The six tracks are not the only ones available, but they are illustrative of the emphasis on professionally preparing yourself for a career.

CONCLUSIONS

A part of becoming a professional is the adherence to the highest ethical standards. This is especially essential for the educator because of the magnitude of the trust and responsibility inherent in the teaching process. Educators must believe in the worth and dignity of all students and must seek to held them realize their potential as effective members of society.

Students are encouraged to inquire, to acquire knowledge, and formulate and to achieve worthy goals. As a student aspiring to a particular career, you need to understand the significance of your commitment when you join a career. While physical education is characterized by extensive training in a body of knowledge and service, communication among colleagues is also essential.

Cross-Sectional and Longitudinal Studies

Every study has some sort of time setting. A study which covers a broad range of phenomena at a single point in time is called a cross-sectional study. For example, Campbell, Converse, and Rodgers study, The Quality of American Life, reports interviews with a national sample of 2,700 households, inquiring as to their satisfactions and dissatisfactions. They found that married people are happier than single people that prosperous people are happier than poor people, and made many other interesting discoveries.

If the study extends over time, describing a trend or making a series of before-and-after observations, it is called a longitudinal study. Thus, Levine and Meyer studied changes in black and white enrolment in Kansas City public schools between 1960 and 1974. They found that schools with a relatively small black enrolment, were likely to "remain desegregated, while schools with a higher percentage of black students became almost totally re-segregated" as a result of what has come to be known as "white flight".

The national public opinion polls are cross-sectional studies, but if the same set of questions is repeated at intervals over a period of years, longitudinal comparisons can be drawn.

Longitudinal studies may be either prospective or retrospective. A retrospective study works backward in time, using data that are already recorded. For example, Wynder and Evarts used hospital records of 605 lung cancer victims and found that all but eight were cigarette smokers. When a retrospective study shows strong evidence of a relationship, the next step often is to see whether a prospective study will confirm the relationship. A prospective study begins with the present and carries observations forward over a period of time. Thus Dorn and Kahn followed the health history of 200,0000 veterans for eleven years, finding that the pack-a-day-or-more smokers were sixteen times as likely to die from lung cancer as were nonsmokers. Prospective studies take a long time to complete and are often very costly, making them one of the least common types of research study.

Sometimes longitudinal conclusions are drawn from cross-sectional studies. A cross-sectional study may show differences between age groups, and this is often interpreted as evidence of changing attitudes or behaviour. For example, numerous studies have shown that young people are more permissible than older people about sex behaviour and drug use. Does this mean that values are changing, and that the values of today's youth will be everybody's values tomorrow? Or is this a life-cycle change, with the young growing more conservative as they grow older? A cross-sectional study will not tell this.

Longitudinal conclusions from cross-sectional studies are often dead wrong. For example, ever since intelligence testing began, cross-sectional comparisons have consistently shown that average IQ seems to peak in early adulthood and declines steadily thereafter. But these surveys were conducted during a period of steadily rising levels of public education. Each thus compared better educated young people with less well educated older people. More recent longitudinal studies measuring IQs of the same persons over a period of years report no consistent decline in IQ until old age, with some aspects of "intelligence" improving and others declining with advancing years. Longitudinal conclusions can only be established by longitudinal studies, even though cross-sectional studies may suggest promising hypotheses.

Methods of Sociological Research

Karl Pearson has remarked, "The unity of all science consists alone in its methods, not in its material. The man who classifies facts of any kind whatever, who sees their mutual relation and describes their sequences, is applying the scientific method and is a man of science."

While scientific methods are basically alike for all sciences, scientific techniques differ, for techniques are the particular ways in which scientific methods are applied to a particular problem. Each science must, therefore, develop a series of techniques which fits the body of material it studies. What are some of the techniques of sociological research?

Laboratory and Field Experiments

All sciences use experiments. In the laboratory experiment materials or people are brought into the laboratory for study. In laboratory experiments with people, people are recruited, assembled, and perhaps paid for engaging in the experiment. Dollard's famous frustration-aggression studies were conducted by assembling a number of students as experimental subjects, supposedly to study the effects of fatigue upon task performance. These students were subjected to intense frustration through prolonged boredom, non-arrival of promised food and games, and other intentional annoyances, while their aggressive responses were catalogued.

The field experiment takes research out to people

instead of bringing people to the research laboratory. A massive field experiment involving vaccination of several million children established the value of Salk polio vaccine. A continuing series of field experiments are seeking to find effective ways of promoting birth control in underdeveloped countries and among disadvantaged groups in the United States.

The concept of any experiment is quite simple: Hold all variables constant except one; cause it to vary and see what happens.

A variable is anything which differs from person to person, group to group, time to time, or place to place— age, education, income, and many others. As an example, suppose we want to know whether abolishing grades would increase learning or increase loafing. To test this by experiment we would need a control group of classes which follow the usual teaching and grading procedures, and an experimental group of classes using whatever experimental procedure is being tested. To "hold all other variables constant", the control and experimental groups would need to be alike in calibre of student, subject studied, quality of teaching, students work load, student's finances, and anything else likely to affect their performance. We would also need a reliable instrument to measure learning outcomes (after reaching agreement upon what learning outcomes were important).

One of the best ways to control all variables is to use control groups. A control group is a group of subjects who are like the observed group in all respects except the variable(s) which we are studying. Failure to use suitable control groups may destroy a study's usefulness. For example, two psychologists examined the Rorschach tests which were given to sixteen Nazi leaders at the time of the Nuremberg war crimes trials, and reported that fifteen of them were "psychopathic" in various degrees. But Miale and Selzer failed to compare the Nazi leader's tests with Rorschach tests from a control group of leaders from other countries or professions. Thus, even if we assume that the analyses are correct, we do not know whether these researchers have uncovered personality characteristics of Nazi leaders, or characteristics of leaders of many kinds. Thus, the study is of limited value.

There are two common ways of setting up experimental and control groups. One is the matched-pair technique. For each person in the experimental group, another person similar in all important variables (such as age, religion, educational, occupation, or anything important to this research) is found and placed in the control group. Another technique is the random-assignment technique, in which statistically random assignments of persons to experimental and control groups are made—such as assigning the first person to the experimental group, the next to the control group, and so on. Suppose we wish to measure the effectiveness of an experimental treatment program for delinquents in a reformatory. Using one technique, we should match each delinquent who received the experimental treatment (experimental group) with another delinquent, matched for other variables thought important, who received only the usual treatment (control group). Using the random-assignment technique, every second (or third, or tenth) delinquent would be assigned to the experimental group upon arrival at the reformatory, with the others becoming the control group. Wherever the researcher is permitted to make assignments in this way, the random-assignment technique is far easier and at least as accurate; but often, when the research situation precludes this technique, the matched-pair technique may be used.

Experiments in sociology face certain difficulties. An experiment involving thousands of people may be prohibitively expensive. It may take years to complete a prospective study. Our values forbid us to use people in any experiments which may injure them. The scientific world reacts strongly in those infrequent instances where human subjects have been used in a hazardous or harmful manner. When people are unwilling to cooperate in an experiment, we cannot force them to do so (although we may occasionally trick them into unconscious cooperation). Furthermore, when people realize that they are experimental subjects, they begin to act differently, and the experiment may be spoiled. Almost any kind of experimental or observational study upon people who know they are being studied will give some interesting findings which may vanish soon after the study is ended.

Planned experiments upon human subjects are most reliable when these subjects do not know the true object of the experiment. They may be given a rationale, a reasonable explanation of what the experimenter is doing, but this rationale may be a harmless but necessary deception which conceals the true purpose of the experiment. For example, McClelland wished to study the effects of alcohol upon normal people in a party atmosphere but told the subjects that he was studying the effects of a party atmosphere upon fantasy, and had them write imaginative stories about pictures he showed them at intervals. But as Kelman points out, the use of deception in social research poses the ethical question of distinguishing between harmless deception and intellectual dishonesty, and may even produce errors in the outcome (subjects may detect the deception and begin second-guessing the researcher!).

Because of all these limitations, social sciences (excepting psychology) make limited use of planned experiments. We use them wherever practical, but depend more heavily on other techniques.

Observational Studies

Observational studies are like experiments in all respects except one: In experiments the scientist arranges for something to happen in order to observe what follows, whereas in the observational study the scientist observes something which happens, or has already happened, by itself. Both rely upon systematic observation under controlled conditions in a search for verifiable sequences and relationships. Both are used in all the sciences, but the procedures for using them vary according to the material being studied. The types of studies which follow are not mutually exclusive, for a study may fit into more than one of these several categories.

Impressionistic Studies. These are informal descriptive and analytic accounts based on observations which are less fully controlled than in more formal studies. They definitely are not a rambling, incoherent recital of whatever one happens to recall having seen, but are an organized presentation of thoughtful, purposeful observations. Suppose a sociologist with a special interest in the family makes a tour of Russia. He or she is alert for information on the Russian family, asks questions about Russian family life of most of the people met, and scans papers and magazines for pictures of family life. The sociologist returns home with some very definite impressions of Russian family life, but they are not based on a systematic, scientifically controlled investigation—on an orderly search of the published literature, on a scientifically constructed sample of informants, and son on. Responsible scholars will call the sociologist's judgments impressions, and will not state them as scientifically established conclusions.

No matter how elaborate, carefully planned, and systematically conducted a study may be, if the recorded data consist of the observer's impressions, it is classed as an impressionistic study. Thus, the Lynds spent many months in "Middletown"; they systematically searched newspaper files, interviewed virtually everyone who held a position of authority or was locally said to be important, and participated in community life. They ended up with a large mass of impressions which were highly perceptive and probably accurate, but not easily verifiable.

Bias is a major hazard in impressionistic research. Studs Terkel and LeMasters spent hundreds of hours listening to working people share their ideas and feelings; then from their huge collection of tapes, notes, and recollections they selected a small portion for publication. This method clearly carries the danger that the observer's feelings will coloured the findings.

Despite this hazard, impressionistic studies are highly useful in social science. They provide many hypotheses and research leads, and suggest many insights which might be overlooked by other methods. The best of the impressionistic studies hold an honoured place in sociological literature.

Statistical Comparative Studies. If the information needed has already been written down somewhere it is sensible to look up the record. Much sociological research consists of looking up recorded statistical facts and comparing and interpreting them. For a simple example, consider the question, "Now that women have greater freedom to lead an interesting and independent life without marriage, are more women remaining single?" While the reasons for remaining single may be a complicated question, the proportion of women remaining single can easily be derived from census data, which show the proportion of single women dropping from 24.3 percent in 1890 to 11.9 percent in 1960, then rising to 14.6 percent in 1975. Many such questions can be answered quickly by checking data in the annual Statistical Abstract of the United States, which summarizes statistics collected by many government and other agencies and should be found in any library. Other questions may require study of more specialized statistical sources, such as the many Special Reports issued by the bureau of the Census.

Many research questions involve a comparison of several kinds of statistical data from several sources. For example, using income data from the U.S. census, Jacobs computed an "index of economic equality" for each American state. Then, using crime statistics from Uniform Crime Reports, he computed an "index of imprisonment probability" a ratio between the number of crimes reported to the police and the number of criminals imprisoned for that type of crime. He hypothesized that imprisonment ratios for property crimes (but not for violent crimes) should be higher wherever economic inequality was greater, and found that his data supported these hypotheses.

Sometimes the researcher must go out and collect the raw statistical data. For example, what factors have produced the fairly large non-student "fringe" which hangs around the edges of major universities? In seeking an answer, Whittaker and Watts administered a standard psychological test to a sample of non-students and to a sample of students at Berkeley. They found the students and non-students to be from similar backgrounds, but found the non-students to be more interested in the arts than practical concerns, more impulsive, less self-disciplined, less integrated in personality, less distinctly masculine or feminine in personality, and more socio-emotionally maladjusted.

Many people "have no use for statistics". Often they do not like statistics because they do not understand them. Statistics, like shotguns, are dangerous when handled by the ignorant, as is shown in Huff's entertaining little book, How to Lie with Statistics. Those who know the uses and abuses of statistics realize that statistics are nothing more or less than organized, measured facts. They are as trustworthy or untrustworthy as is the scientific method of the person who compiles them. To reject statistics is but a way of rejecting facts.

Sociologists make a great many comparative statistical studies. As almost any kind of research is likely to involve statistical organization and comparison of facts at some point or other, the sociologist must be something of a statistician, and citizens who hope to be intelligently aware of the world they live in must have some understanding of statistical interpretation, lest they be duped by every clever propagandist in sight.

Questionnaire and Interview Studies. Some times the facts we need are not recorded anywhere, and we can find them only by asking people. Thus, Ferree interviewed 135 married women with elementary school children, and reported that the full-time housewives were considerably more "dissatisfied with life" than those who were employed, while six large national interview studies found no consistent relationship. Questionnaire and interview studies are systematic ways of asking questions under scientific controls. A questionnaire is filled out by the informant personality; an interview schedule is filled out by a trained interviewer who asks the questions of the informant. Both sociologist should be able to avoid. The informants may not understand the question; they may pick an answer even though they do not have any firm opinion on the matter; they may give an "acceptable" answer rather than the real one; or they may be swayed by the way the question is worded. A survey may also give false conclusions because the sample of persons surveyed is not a representative cross section of the population. If too few of the questionnaires are completed and returned, the sample is not a representative cross section and the findings are unreliable. Thus, The Hite Report, a best-selling popular book which claims to give the inside story on women's sex lives, is based upon a 3 percent questionnaire return, making it utterly worthless as research. Questionnaire and interview studies, like other types of research, must be used by scientists who are aware of such pitfalls if the research is to be reliable.

Even though questionnaire and interview studies have a margin of error, they may still be useful, for they are more reliable than guesswork. Public officials seldom take a position on a public issue without first reviewing public opinion polls and legislators often delay casting a vote on an important bill until they receive the latest survey of voter opinion from their districts. Educational administrators planning course offerings and statesmen responsible for foreign policy find questionnaire and interview study data useful.

Pure and Applied Sociology

A distinction between pure and applied science is drawn in every scientific field. Pure science is a search for knowledge, without primary concern for its practical use. Applied science is the search for ways of using scientific knowledge to solve practical problems. A biochemist who seeks to learn how a cell absorbs food or how a cell ages and grows old is working as a pure scientist. If this biochemist then tries to find some substance or procedure which will control the aging process, this is applied science. A sociologist making a study of "the social structure of a slum neighbourhood" is working as a pure scientist; if this is followed by a study of "how to prevent delinquency in a slum neighbourhood", this is applied science. Many people view sociology entirely as an applied science—trying to solve social problems. Properly viewed, it is both a pure and an applied science. For unless a science is constantly searching for more basic knowledge, its "practical applications of knowledge" are not likely to be very practical.

Practical applications of sociological knowledge are not widely appreciated. Some sociologists are employed by corporations, government bureaus, and social agencies, often in evaluation research but sometimes in administration. Sociologists are sometimes consulted by legislative committees planning new legislation. But the private citizen rarely bases his or her social decisions upon sociological knowledge. If we want to know how to fertilize artichokes, we generally collect some scientific data before deciding. But how are social-policy decisions made? Usually by balancing the political clout of the various organized interest groups which are pressuring their congressmen.

On many social questions such as the causes and treatment of crime and delinquency, drug and alcohol addiction, sex offences, the causes and consequences of racial discrimination, or the adjustment of the family to a changing society, there is considerable scientific knowledge, but this knowledge is rejected by many persons who prefer their prejudices. As a nation, we have only begun to apply scientific methods to our thinking about social issues.

Popular Sociology

A great deal of sociology material gets into print through the agency of people who are not sociologists. The popular magazines are studded with articles on crime, family life, sex, education, suburbia, social class—practically every sociological topic imaginable. This is popular sociology—treatment of sociological topics, nearly always by writers without much formal sociological training, and aimed at a popular audience. Popular sociology at its worst is seen in articles like the "sex-and-sin" exposés upon which certain men's magazines dwell so fondly. Such articles are generally descriptively inaccurate, with a total lack of the interpretative analysis which would fit the facts into a relevant social context. At the opposite pole are many writers who do a fairly creditable job of popularizing sociological findings. For example, Stoner and Parke's All God's Children, a study of new religious cults, is written by non-sociologists, but the authors are careful, observant, sensitive journalists.

"Pop sociology" often contains inaccuracies and instances of misplaced emphasis, doubtful interpretation, oversimplification, and too-sweeping generalization. Yet it is likely that popular understanding of sociological topics has been greatly increased by such writers.

Why is not popular sociology written by professional sociologists? For the same reason that popular science is usually written by journalists, rather than by scientists. Popular writing is a special skill which few scientists or professors have mastered. Furthermore, the scientist's passion for accuracy and for a careful qualification of all statements is a positive handicap in popular writing. Unwillingness to oversimplify, to over-dramatize, or to indulge in grandly sweeping generalization all make the professional's writing more accurate but less exciting. Sociologists write for the scholarly audience while journalists popularize sociology, more or less accurately, for the public.

The Roles of the Sociologist

What is the proper task of the sociologist? Is it merely to observe human action with the calm, detached curiosity of the ecologist who counts the lemmings as they dive into the sea? Or should the sociologist plunge into social action? Should the professor of sociology encourage students to develop a detached understanding of social phenomena or inspire them to man the barricades for social reform? What is the proper role for the sociologist in a changing society?

The Sociologist as Research Scientist

Like all scientists, sociologists are concerned with both collection and using knowledge. They share in these tasks in various ways.

Conducting Scientific Research. As a scientist, the sociologist's foremost task is to discover and organize knowledge about social life. A number of full-time research sociologists are employed by universities, government agencies, foundations, or corporations, and many sociologists divide their time between teaching and research. Many university sociologists are engaged in "funded" research, with all or part of their salaries and their research expenses paid from research grants made by government agencies, foundations, or corporations. These grants are made to sociologists who submit an acceptable proposal for research on a particular topic. Since little research can be conducted without research funds, this gives the funding agencies great power to influence the direction of sociological research.

Radical critics of sociology (including some sociologists) claim that, behind a facade of ethical neutrality and objectivity, sociologists have prostituted their research talents to the support of the interests of the funding agencies, and have thus supported militarism, racism, and other forms of oppression.

Whether sociological research has been widely corrupted in this manner may be debated. What is indisputable is that problems of bias and partisanship are present in all research, and that research findings are often helpful to the interests of some people and damaging to the interests of other people. Even the definition of a research problem may carry an implicit bias. For example, if we state a research problem as, "What characteristics of poor people contribute to their poverty?", we imply that the "blame" rests mainly on the poor people themselves; but if we define the problem as, "What social arrangements produce poverty?", then the blame is placed upon "society."

Throughout most of the history of sociology, sociologists were often accused of being radical subversives whose research and teaching were a threat to established institutions and vested interests. Many older sociologists today, still bearing the scars of the anti-Communist witch-hunts of the 1950s, are puzzled and hurt when students and younger sociologists accuse them of having been lackeys of capitalistic oppression all their lives! But the question of the responsibility of the scientist to society is as old as science itself, and will not soon be settled.

Correcting Popular Nonsense. Another task of the sociologist as a scientist is to clear away the intellectual rubbish of misinformation and superstition which clutters so much of our social thinking. Sociologists have helped to bury a great deal of nonsense about heredity, race, class, sex differences, deviation and nearly every other aspect of behaviour. It is due partly to the findings of sociology that today we rarely hear an educated person argue that the white race in innately superior, that women are intellectually inferior to men, that behaviour traits are inherited, or that rural people are less "immoral" than urbanities—ideas which nearly every educated person accepted a half century ago. By helping replace superstition and misinformation with accurate knowledge about human behaviour sociologists are perhaps performing their most important function.

Making Sociological Predictions. Although the track record of sociologists in making social predictions is not impressive, someone must make social predictions. Every policy decision is based upon certain assumptions about the present and future state of the society. A legislator who says, "We need more severe penalties to curb drug pushing" is predicting that more severe penalties actually will curb the narcotics business without creating even greater problems. Another legislator .who says, "Legalize marijuana" is making a set of predictions about the consequences of this action. Thus every policy recommendation inevitably implies a set of assumptions and predictions. What sort of predictions do sociologists offer? Here are a few samples,. offered without explanation or documentation at this point, as examples of the kind of predictions sociologists can make:

The trend toward employment of women will continue until most women are working for most of their married lives.

Birth rates will fall to approach death rates, or death rates will rise to approach birth rates.

Despite some experimentation with alternatives, the monogamous nuclear family will continue to be the basic family type in the United States.

The present popularity of jeans and casual clothing among young people will be followed by a return to high-style clothing.

The recent trend toward early retirement will soon be replaced by efforts to lengthen the work career.

Most social science prediction consists not of predicting specific developments, as the astronomer predicts an eclipse, but of forecasting the general pattern of trends and changes which seem most probable. All such predictions or forecasts should be offered with a certain humility, for no certainty attends them. Instead, social scientists offer them as the best, most informed guesses available upon which to base out policy decisions and expectations for the future.

The Sociologist as Policy Consultant

Sociological prediction can also help to estimate the probable effects of a social policy. Every social policy decision is a prediction. A policy is begun in the hope that it will produce a desired effect (e.g., narrow the educational gap between poor and more prosperous children). Policies have often failed because they embodied unsound assumptions and predictions. Sociologists can help to predict the effects of a policy, and thus contribute to the selection of policies which achieve the intended purposes. For example:

What effects do brotherhood propaganda and "education for brotherhood" efforts have on race prejudices? (None.)

What effect does dropping out of high school have upon a youth's future earnings? (Little or none, when other factors are equal.)

What would be the effect of intensified law enforcement upon campus marijuana use? (Little or no reduction, with aggravation of other student-police problems).

Would lower birthrates and a small-family norm increase marital happiness? (Yes; there is research evidence that smaller families are better in every way).

Would publishing the names of juvenile delinquents help to reduce delinquency? (No; it would more likely increase it).

Would the suppression of obscene literature help to reduce sex crimes and sex immorality? (Our limited evidence suggests that it would not).

These are a few of the many social-policy questions which sociologist could help to settle. So far our society has not generally accorded the sociologist a status as technical expert on social-policy matters. The image of the sociologist as a professional bleeding heart, so often reflected in the popular press, does not help the public to visualize the sociologist as a technical expert. Congressional committees, however, often consult sociologists and other social scientist when holding hearings on proposed legislation. In some areas, especially in criminology and race relations, the conclusions of sociologists (and other social scientists) have had considerable influence. It was, in considerable part, the findings of sociologists and psychologists which led the United States Supreme Court to rule that "segregated schools are inherently unequal".

The Sociologist as Technician

Today sociologists are increasingly finding employment with government departments, corporations, hospitals, large welfare agencies, and other large organizations. Aside from research, they are engaged in planning and conducting community action programs; advising on public relations, employee relations, problems of morale or of "intergroup relations" within the organization; working on human relations problems of many sorts. The "staff sociologist" is found in all kinds of large organizations. Often this person has specialized in social psychology, industrial sociology, urban or rural sociology, or the sociology of complex organizations.

Recently, the term clinical sociologist has appeared to describe the work of the sociologist as technician. To some extent, this is a new name for what sociologists have been doing for a long time, but it also includes a considerable broadening of the range of sociologist's efforts to be useful in society.

In such positions the sociologist is working as an applied scientist. He or she has been engaged to use scientific knowledge in pursuing certain values—a harmonious and efficient working force, an attractive public image of the industry, or an effective community action program. This role raises a question of ethics. When a sociologist accepts employment as a technician, pursuing values chosen by an employer, has scientific integrity been compromised? To take an extreme example, there is evidence that gambling operators engaged social scientists to find out why people do or do not gamble, so that the operators could learn how to attract more customers. Would this be a form of scientific prostitution?

The radical critics of "establishment sociology" charge that sociologists have "sold out" whenever they serve as technicians or research scholars in any kind of effort to maintain or improve the efficiency of the government, military, capitalistic, or welfare establishments. Thus, not only are sociologists (if any) working in war-related activities condemned, but even sociologists working in programs to improve the health of poor children in Mississippi, to increase agricultural output in Peru, or to teach birth control in village India are accused of supporting "oppression". This is the classic view of the revolutionist—any attempt to make the present system work better, or to help people find better lives within the system is "oppressive" because it helps to perpetuate the system.

There is no simple answer to the question of what clinical appointments it is proper for the sociologist to accept. Each sociologist's answer will be found partly in the prevailing views of the academic world at that moment and partly in his or her own conscience.

The Sociologist as Teacher

Teaching is the major career of most sociologists. In addition to the concerns and problems of teaching in any field, the problem of value neutrality versus value commitment is a particularly acute question. For example, in a course on "poverty", should the sociologist supervise an objective study of facts, theories, and policies—possibly sympathetic but as objective as possible? Or should he or she design the course to produce dedicated advocates of a particular action program? Should the sociologist seek to convert students to conservatism, liberal reformisms, or revolutionary activism? For some decades the ethics of university teaching have demanded that the teacher refrain from all conscious "indoctrination", but this question is now under spirited debate.

The Sociologist and Social Action

Scientists seek to discover knowledge. Should scientists also tell the society how this knowledge should be used? For example, the geneticists already know something about human heredity, and before very long it may be possible to control the genetic make-up of babies, and "order" babies according to a specifications list. Who should decide what sort of baby should go to whom? The scientists? The parents? The government?

The basic question is whether science—specifically sociology—should be value-free. For example, sociologists know some things about population growth, race relations, urban development, and many other matters involving questions of public policy. Should sociologists become public advocates of birth-control programs, legalized abortion, women's liberation, legalized marijuana, racial integration, and many other programs which they may consider socially desirable?

Early sociologists gave an emphatic "yes" to this question. Without an adequate foundation of scientific knowledge, they rushed to support all sorts of public policies they believed wise. Between 1920 and 1940, many sociologists shifted to the view that sociology should be a more nearly "pure" science, discovering knowledge but not attempting to decree how it should be used. They sought to build sociology on the model of physics or chemistry, as a value-free science. As such, it should be committed to no values except those of free scientific inquiry. Sociologists generally avoided involvement in controversial issues and sought the status of "pure" social scientists.

Sociology today, in common with all the other social sciences, has some members who insist that, both individually and as an academic discipline, sociologists should openly and publicly support the "radical reconstruction of society". This question is receiving much attention in sociological literature. Whether sociology should be value-free is an unsettled question, but sociologists are agreed upon the following propositions:

(1) Sociologists should show the relationships between values. In short, sociologists may say, "If this is what you want, here is what you must do to get it." If stable, enduring marriages are more important than happiness in marriage, then divorce should be made more difficult; if happy

marriages represent the more important value, then fairly easy divorce should permit the unhappily married to separate and try again. If we wish to arrest urban blight and suburban sprawl, some private property rights will have to be sacrificed. If we wish to clean up polluted rivers we must be prepared to spend a lot of tax money in doing so. Sociologists may clarify what value sacrifices must be made if we wish to attain certain other values.

(2) A sociologist as an individual may properly make value judgments, support causes, and join reform movements, like any other citizen. As a scientist, the sociologist may not know whether television violence is harmful to children, and therefore make no public recommendations; but as a parent will make a decision according to his or her personal beliefs and values. As a scientist, the sociologist may not be able to say whether gambling or marijuana should be forbidden, but as a citizen is free to express opinions and support personal value judgments.

Beyond this there is no complete agreement among sociologists concerning what role they should assume. Most sociologists have some firm opinions on what policies society should follow and are in considerable agreement with one another upon many of these policies. Possibly the time will come when the social policies which seem best to most sociologists will also seem best to the rest of the society.

The Study of Sociology

Students are sometimes delighted to find in sociology (or another social science) evidence that some of their parents fondest beliefs are outmoded superstitions. But when they find evidence that their own beliefs are scientifically unfounded, their reaction to this correction may not differ greatly from that of their parents. To separate sense from nonsense is one of the objectives of sociology. Only those who are willing and able to subject their beliefs, assumptions, and practices to objective scientific scrutiny will gain much from the study of any of the social sciences.

The Use of Concepts in Sociology

Every field of study makes the student memorize many words to which the field attaches special meanings. This is not an ideal ritual; it is done because precise concepts are necessary. First, we need carefully expressed concepts to carry on a scientific discussion. How would you explain machinery to a person who had no concept of "wheel"? How useful to a specialist would a patient's medical history be if her physician had recorded it in the language of the layman? The several dozen sociological concepts which will harass the student are necessary for a clear discussion of social phenomena. Secondly, the formulation of concepts leads to increased knowledge. Some accurate descriptive knowledge must be organized before a concept can be framed. Then the analysis and criticism of this new concept point up the gaps and errors in present knowledge. Use of the concept often calls attention to facts and relationships which studying migration Park framed the concept of the marginal man who is on the fringes of two groups or two ways of life while fully belonging to neither. The use of this concept quickly led to the recognition that there were many kinds of marginal persons—the person of mixed racial ancestry, who belongs clearly to neither race; the supervisor, who is not clearly either "management" or "labour"; the ambitious climber, no longer in the working class yet not securely a middle-class person; and many others. Sound concepts like that of the marginal man lead to increased knowledge.

Most of the concepts of sociology are expressed in words which also have a popular meaning, just as the term order has one meaning in zoology, another at the restaurant table, and still another at a law-and-order political rally. Every science appropriates some common words and makes them into scientific concepts by giving them a specific definition. Sociology is no exception.

Careers in Sociology

A student who becomes interested in a subject may wonder what possibilities it holds for a career. A combination of courses which constitutes an undergraduate major or minor in sociology is not, in itself, preparation for a professional career as a sociologist. Undergraduate majors and minors are useful mainly as background preparation for other careers: (1) In social work, the better jobs demand a graduate degree in social work, and usually recommend a strong undergraduate major in sociology. (2) In the professions—medicine, law, engineering—it has been found that undergraduate social science courses are useful. (3) Secondary schools present some demand for sociology teachers. (4) Civil service positions often include undergraduate sociology among the acceptable educational qualifications for a wide variety of positions in lower and middle brackets. (5) Sociologists are employed in small numbers by industry, trade associations, labour unions, foundations, and in fairly large numbers by research organizations, in a wide variety of positions, very often in the administration and conduct of research. (6) Newly emerging careers are to be found in many sorts of action programs—local human relations councils, fair employment practices commissions, economic opportunity programs, foreign aid programs, and many others. Such careers are too new to have developed any rigidly standardized courses of professional preparation, but sociology majors are often sought for these positions.

An M.A. degree is sometimes sufficient to obtain a teaching position at a junior college or community college, but promotions and university appointments usually require a Ph.D., which is even more necessary for a career in sociology than it is in the other sciences. Among those scientists with enough "professional standing in the scientific community" to be listed in the 1970 National Register of Scientific and Technical Personnel, a doctor's degree was held by 76 percent of the sociologists, as compared with 66 percent of the psychologists, 42 percent of the economists, 41 percent of the physicists, 36 percent of the chemists; the sociologists were exceeded only by the anthropologists, 90 percent of whom held a doctorate. Of all sociologists, about 84 percent are employed by educational institutions, with the remainder scattered among many employers, mainly government agencies and private foundations. Teaching is the major activity of 58 percent of sociologists, with 22 percent in management and administration, most often management and administration of research.

Until recently the demand exceeded the supply of persons with doctorates in practically all fields. About 1970, curbacks in government funding and in weapons and aerospace research cost many Ph.D.'s their jobs, especially in the physical sciences and engineering. Meanwhile the rate of growth of college enrolments began to slow down, while graduate school output of Ph.D.'s was still rising. Consequently, the employment outlook for graduating Ph.D.'s for the decade of the 1980s is mixed. About 800 openings for new sociology Ph.D.'s a year are anticipated in the 1976-1985 decade. Superior sociology Ph.D.'s will probably get good jobs; mediocre ones may have difficulty.

For most students, sociology will not be a career but merely part of their general liberal arts education. Whatever career they enter, they will be members of a society, residents in a community, participants in many groups, and carriers of the culture to the next generation. The study of sociology may aid them to fill with greater insight these varied roles which are their destiny.

The descriptive method of research deals with the sciences, physical or social, and performs certain essential functions such as description, explanation, prediction and control. It has to adopt various methods for realising these functions. The descriptive method is one such used by scientists, particularly the social scientists. The descriptive method is the simplest one and is applicable to a number of social problems. It is essentially a fact-finding approach related largely to the present and abstracting generalisations arrived at by a cross-sectional study of the current situation. It comprises mainly collection of data; but mere collection is not research. So, the descriptive method to some extent also interprets the data. The social scientist sees to it that his research finding is arrived at after following methodical processes and procedures like observation, explanation, interpretation and generalisation of the data gathered.

As a matter of fact there are multifarious problems in society and the social problems which crop up then and there lend themselves to the descriptive study. The problems in the social fields are larger in number than can be studied through the application of this method. The types of problems covered here include describing the characteristics of communities, establishing the proportion of people in a specified population who hold certain views or attitudes or who behave in certain ways, and discovering of testing whether certain variables are associated. Some specific trend or prediction studied may also fall under this category; whether the popularity of a sportsman is declining over a period of time or how many people will attend a national level football match.

There is no hard and fast rule that the descriptive method has to be limited to any one method of data collection. There are no bounds or any restriction on the employment of methods. They may make use of any or all of the methods like observation, questionnaire, interviewing and scaling techniques used by social scientist. Although descriptive studies may be a wide range of techniques, this does not mean that they are characterised by the flexibility that marks exploratory studies. The procedure to be used in a descriptive study must be carefully planned. Because the aim is to obtain complete and accurate information, the design must make much provision for protection against work involved in descriptive studies frequently concerns economy of research, this effort is extremely necessary and significant. The major steps such as formulating the objectives of the study, designing the methods of data collection, selecting the sample, collecting and checking the data and analysing the results are the main steps in a descriptive investigation.

The investigator must take utmost care of the limitations that are found in this method. The researcher may make description an end in itself as the research is essentially creative and demands the discovery of facts in order to lead to a solution of the problem.

Historical Research

In common parlance, we come across people jokingly saying, "history is a mystery". But in reality, it cannot be considered so because history tells about the very concrete past or actual happenings in the past with a bit of exaggeration as the historians have the legitimate licence to make their narration colourful and inspiring. It will of course, be futile to expect only facts as the narration is affected by the writer's bias and prejudices.

Historically, research in our civilisation has been profoundly influenced by early discoveries. The discovery of fire, the wheel, numbers and the alphabet, paper and the process of printing; the development of metals and agriculture; and the use of steam and electricity have all been milestones in the development and refinement of civilisation. More recently have come the use of atomic power and the penetration of outer space, which in a very real sense are the culmination of long years of research and development.

History

History is a meaningful record of human achievements. It is not merely a list of chronological events but a truthful, integrated account of the relationship between persons, events, time and places. We use history to understand the past, and to understand the present in the light of past events and developments. Historical analysis may be directed toward an individual, an idea, a movement, or an institution. However, none of these objects of historical observation can be considered in isolation. People cannot be subjected to historical investigation without some consideration of their interaction with the ideas, movements or institutions of their times. The focus merely determines the points of emphasis toward which historians direct their attention.

"Historia" is a Greek term from which the term "history" has been derived and history can be rightly called the "present mirror" for the past events, achievements, political or social changes, etc. It reflects the wholesome picture of the life of the men who lived in yester-years.

In early days, human history included a study of the past problem. The main task of historians was to collect information about the past events and to analyse them correctly. History or historical books, therefore, mainly dealt with the life and deeds of important persons. In history books, record of kings or their army commanders and great men are also found, with a view to interpreting past events.

A new method of research, known as the "historical method", came into being. In the social sciences the historical method is used as an aid to visualising society as a dynamic organism.

Human society is an eternally dynamic structure. History is a record of changing processes. This is why, in social sciences, a study of the social processes, is so revealing and important. According to Hans Garth, "Every model of social structure implies a model of socio-historical change; history consists of changes which social structures undergo". In the historical study of a social structure, the casual relation between the various aspects becomes known. The current structure, culture, folkways and social moves and organisation of any social group are resultants of its past forces, that is, its history and evolution.

The knowledge about these processes enables us to anticipate their future structure. No social change takes place in void; it is a result of past forces and will give rise to future forces. Accordingly, in order to understand effectively any social group or institution, it has to be studied in its perspective. History enlarges the range of observed phenomena, affords a sense of mutuality of institutions and suggests conditioning factors in contemporary life.

In this way, the social scientist studies the past to gain a better understanding of the present state of affairs. Though the contemporary ethos and culture of any society is quite different from its past character, yet the seeds of the present are in the past and the contemporary modes and mores of a society are nothing but an evolution of the forces working in the past.

When a research is conducted on the basis of historical data, the researcher is said to have followed the historical approach. At times, it would appear that all research is historical in its nature because, to a very large extent, research depends upon observations which are non-repetitive. Historical facts cannot be repeated in an accurate fashion as can be done in laboratory observations.

Historical research involves very intensive use of library material and requires patience on the part of the researcher to believe into the historical records. It is essential that the problem treated with this approach is historical in nature. Only such problems as are based on historical records can be investigated by following this approach.

The historical approach to research, may or may not be formulated depending upon the nature of investigation. In historical records, an attempt it usually made to establish the hypothesis formulated by a researcher. The interpretation of research data entirely depends upon the researcher himself and shall depend upon how objectively he carries out his job of interpreting the historical evidence. Therefore, it is very hard to disprove a hypothesis of the researcher and on the other hand he may conveniently make data bear upon his conclusions.

Modern Historians

Few modern historians cling to the "great-man theory of history," and a few give merely episodic or dramatic fragments of events. Most modern historians present a cross-section of a level of life and events, of similarities and common traits, of the collective life of mankind. In brief, they are interested in the social process as a seamless web. They realise that a collection of historical events about politics, law, economic activities and development, religion and other aspects of life would not constitute a history of mankind. The social process as a whole must also be synthesized and explained.

Sources of Historical Data

Historical research should be encouraged because it is related to the heritage of the field. No established profession has depth, traditions, customs, or a present without a history. This heritage should be recorded and preserved for future generations. The origin, growth, and development of the field; the problems faced and solved;

the cultural forces exerted, the movements that have waned and persisted; the changes in implements, facilities, and costumes; the thoughts and deeds of the pioneers and leaders who shaped the profession over the years; and many other factors are subjects for historical research.

We may generally confine ourselves to three major sources of historical information:

(i) documents and various historical sources to which the historian has access;

(ii) materials of cultural history and of analytical history; and

(iii) personal sources i.e., authentic observers and witness.

When, how and under what circumstances, to use any or all of these sources depends a great deal upon the description of the student, his interests, the scope of his study and the availability of these sources.

Many of the sources indispensable for adequate knowledge of the past include diaries, memoirs, concessions, autobiographies, secret archives, diplomatic agreements, uncoordinated statistical material, under-cover trade agreements, cold-storaged invention and countless other data.

The related literature provides the main source of information in historical research. The document serve as the reports of events consisting of impressions made on some human brain by past events and consciously or deliberately recorded for the purpose of transmitting information. The evaluation of documents is of crucial importance to enable the researcher to place each bit of information in its proper perspective and draw sound conclusions. The evaluation of historical evidence is usually known as, "historical criticism," which is generally divided into two groups, namely,

(1) external criticism or Henristics which means inciting to find out or guiding in discovery, and

(2) internal criticism or hermaneutics or interpretative criticism. The main aim of these two types of criticism is to pronounce whether a given idea is acceptable as a fact or not. Events, occurrences, and happenings as presented in the records may or may not conform to reality, for they might have been distorted, twisted or misinterpreted. Thus, through these methods and authenticity and credibility of the data is tested.

External criticism is concerned with the genuineness of the document, i.e., testing the authenticity and credibility of the data. In other words, external criticism deals with data relating to form and appearance rather than meaning or contents. External criticism is sometimes called lower criticism because it is a preliminary preparatory step providing the data to be used in the second phase known as internal criticism. In testing the genuineness of a document the problem of external criticism involves the question of authorship and his qualifications as a reporter, factors, or conditions that may have influenced the production of the document, such as time, place, purpose, and circumstances of compositions and the extent to which the document reads true to the original. In determining the truth and value of the document, the researcher has to go into the question of authorship, his personality, character, position, general qualifications as reporter, special qualification or disqualification as a reporter of the matter, interest in the events, his technical knowledge for learning and reporting the events, the ability and technique, method of writing the document from memory, after consultation with others, the data and year of documentation and such other details.

On the contrary, internal criticism evaluates the accuracy and value or worth of the statements within the document. In other words, it is testing the credibility of the data. This process is also called higher criticism. A historical researcher must put his documentary evidence to the test of truthfulness as well as competence. At times, many authentic or genuine documents may not be completely accurate or truthful and require internal criticism in the form of textual criticism as well as investigation of such factors as the competence, good faith, position and bias of the author of the document. Internal criticism involves a scientific examination of the relevance of the data, correction of errors, and rejection of the information that is found wanting.

There are two types of internal criticism: (1) negative criticism; and (ii) positive criticism. The negative criticism examines the circumstances and surroundings in which a person wrote the document, whether he was in a position to ascertain the truth and to reveal the real story and whether he was guided by motives or bias. Positive criticism seeks to find out whether the contents of the documents are true or otherwise. In historical research, both negative and positive criticism are essential.

History has attained a certain degree of maturity as a social science. The problem that remains is that of making more explicit as a matter of practice the status already recognised in principle, of making investigation more penetrating, analysis more precise, and demonstration more rigorous. This is a problem that history, in company with other sciences, has always to face.

Adequacy of Historical Data

The historical data may be regarded as reliable and adequate only.

(i) when it is presented as a complex of social forces;

(ii) when social phenomena meaningfully depict intricate social processes; and

History can be regarded as a social science that needs little argument. Historians have long been aware of their responsibility as social scientists. They have consistently affirmed the necessity of analysing historical data rigorously. For some generations, the practice as well as the philosophy of historians have reflected a scientific spirit; and historical studies exhibit modes of thinking directly traceable to the methods of social science.

Steps in the Historical Method

The historical method studies the problems in a broad manner. This study involves certain steps which are enumerated as follows:

1. The selection of the problem
2. The collection of data
3. The historical evaluation and analysis

Precautions for Persons adopting the Historical Method

A person who adopts the historical method has to be cautious. He should safeguard against certain drawbacks and defects so that study may not be spoiled by lack of objectivity or failure of presenting historical facts in proper perspective. The precautions to be taken are enumerated below:

1. Over-simplification;
2. Over-generalisation;
3. Failure to interpret the terms of the past;

Advantages of the Historical Approach

The advantages of the historical approach are, of course, numerous and, after almost things under the sun and above occur in a cyclic fashion with a bit of expected or unexpected changes because change is the only reality of the cosmos.

(i) Some problems are such that they can be investigated only by this approach and may not offer themselves to other approaches. Therefore, the historical approach fills is in a big gap of making the research possible and also meaningful on the problems that would otherwise have remained unexplored.

(ii) Secondly, historical data are not repeatable under any circumstances and, therefore, the historical approach serves as a ready-to-hand method to the researcher whose problems depend on historical observations. It is fairly easy to repeat observations in laboratories under controlled conditions but this cannot be done in case of historical data.

(iii) Thirdly, historical records provide very useful information that goes a long way towards the solution of a research problem. As already said, the researcher is compelled to fall back upon the past since he cannot create these afresh and hence it is highly advantageous to follow the historical approach where the use of time series data is unavoidable in any case.

Limitations

The historical approach is not free from limitations. The main drawbacks of this approach are:

(i) Non-matching situations,

(ii) Over-generalisation, and

(iii) Subjective interpretations.

i. Non-Matching Situations

A serious shortcoming of the historical approach is that a past situation cannot be matched to an existing situation. A past situation might have been influenced by social, economic and political factors which are no longer the and hence present comparability of the past to the present can easily be questioned. This is more so in social sciences where it is very difficult to keep the socio-economic conditions and other dimensions of the problems under control.

(ii) Over-Generalisations

Secondly, it has been observed that researchers with this approach tend to overgeneralise their results. This sometimes leads to implausible explanations and inaccurate specifications of the research problem. Sometimes also, the results may be generalised beyond reasonable limits and these may lead to misunderstanding of historical process.

(iii) Subjective Interpretation

Thirdly, there are great possibilities of a researcher adopting a subjective interpretation in order to validate his hypothesis. The loss of objectivity in such cases can lead to considerable inaccuracies in research findings. In social sciences, the scope for subjective interpretation is large because socio-economic variables are complex in nature and can be interpreted in different ways. In spite of the honest efforts of a researcher circumstances may compel him to go in for subjective interpretations at the cost of objective analysis only to defend his findings which could otherwise be challenged or disproved by other researchers.

Limitations may also arise in the writing of history itself because

(i) historians cannot write history life-size,

(ii) not all happenings in time and space can be known at the time of writing, and

(iii) personal bias and private interpretations often enter unconsciously, even when honest attempts are made to select pertinent facts, to arrange them consistently, and to place them in a coherent and true frame of reference.

However, it should be observed that this approach cannot be dispensed with as a large number of problems cannot be investigated in the absence of historical research. Many a time, it would be desirable for researchers to look into historical records to have better insight into their own investigation.

It is quite obvious that history repeats itself with the same reflection and proportion in our own time. The behavioural pattern does not depend upon the past or the future but on the present. Modern historians are interested in the cultural changes. There always exists a connecting link between experiences and present attitudes and values. Moreover, the historical events are closely interwoven with the social life of men. It is natural that a novice doing historical research may ask: "Why should a man concern himself with old records compiled and written long ago by persons of varied interests and points of view?"

The question of whether or not the historical method is scientific has often been debated. Generally, early historians wrote history more as an instrument of propaganda; their purpose was to glorify the cause espoused, whether it be the state, the church, a given organisation or institution, or the perpetuation of the memory of a public servant or professional pioneer.

The contention is made, however, that modern historians exhibit scientific characteristics in that they critically and objectively investigate their source materials; they formulate and evaluate hypotheses; they make explanations, tentatively at least of the occurrence of events or conditions. But unlike scientists, historians cannot test their hypotheses by direct experimentation; they cannot employ controlled observation. Original conditions cannot be repeated; history cannot be re-enacted. The primary function of science is to get at the true facts, or probabilities, as precisely as possible, by weighing all the available evidence. Historical evidence can be evaluated.

Actually, the scholar of physical education need not be unduly concerned as to whether the historical method is or is not scientific. It is sufficient to know that certain sources of evidence are available for historical study, that these sources can be appropriately evaluated, that generalisations regarding the past can be made and that hypotheses relative to the future can be proposed. The method of history must be understood and rigidly followed if historical studies are to be worthy of note.

Evaluation of Historical Materials

External Criticism

1. Who is the author?
2. Was the document written by a ghost writer or by a genuine person?
3. What were the qualifications of the author?
4. Is a particular item of equipment, piece of apparatus, costume, or other professional artificial authentic?

Internal Criticism

1. Is the meaning of the words the same?
2. Is the author writing seriously?
3. Is the author expressing his or her real beliefs?
4. How soon after the event was the document written?
5. Was the author biased in any way?
6. Are written sources evaluated with an understanding of the times and conditions under which they were produced?

Survey Method

Modern society is beset with so many problems and every department clamours for solutions, rectifications, and reformation. Sufficient information and necessary details about these problems may not be available in records, files and other sources in the concerned areas or departments. Hence, a study of population by applying personal contact, interviews or other techniques. These are generally known as social surveys.

The social survey plays a predominant role in regulating the different aspects of the socio-economic sphere and in all other disciplines including physical education. The social survey is an important tool or technique employed extensively in all social science disciplines to gather evidence relating to social problems. It is a process by which quantitative facts about a social phenomenon are collected to contribute to the solution of immediate problems. The survey approach is followed in studying local as well as state and national problems. The survey method helps us to build a body of facts and figures which possess greater significance and may do a great deal to solve immediate problems including those in the realm of physical education.

Survey research is that branch of social scientific investigation that studies large and small populations, by selecting and studying samples chosen from the population, to discover the relevant incidence, distribution and interrelation of sociological and psychological variables. Surveys covered by this definition are often called sample surveys, probably because survey research developed as a separate research activity along with the development and improvement of sampling procedures. The definition also links population and sample.

Survey research is interested in the current assessment of the characteristics of whole populations of the people. Sample surveys attempt to determine the incidence, distribution and interrelations among sociological and psychological variables.

The nature of survey research as a social science is revealed by the nature of its variables which can be classified as sociological facts and opinion and attitudes. Sociological facts are attributes of individuals that spring from their membership in social groups. Psychological variables include opinions, attitudes and behaviour. The survey researcher is not only interested in the sociological variables but is also primarily interested in what people think and what they do.

Personal interviews, mailed questionnaires, panel and controlled observations are the usual methods of obtaining information. The survey research approach has contributed much to the methodology of the social sciences. Its most important contributions have been in the sphere of rigorous sampling procedures, in the overall design and implementation of the design of studies, in the unambiguous specification of the research problem and in the analysis of the data. Survey researchers use a flowchart which starts with the objectives of the survey, lists each step to be taken in the survey and ends with the final report.

The term "survey" has been derived from "veeir" and "sur" which means "over" and "see" respectively. Therefore, the word "survey" literally means "seeing over" a particular thing from a high place. But this term has come to acquire a specific connotation for social sciences and other sciences too. In natural sciences, this term is generally used for "measurement" and in social sciences it connotes a technique of collection of data or information through interview, questionnaire, etc.

Some scholars are of the view that the term survey can be used only when a direct contact is made between the investigator and the subject. But in reality, it is not so. It includes the collection of data through any method such as interviews, questionnaires, library or books etc.

In the survey method, the data are not collected on

the basis of the experiments carried out under the artificial and controlled conditions. The researcher may in person go to concerned field or area, collect data, frame hypotheses, draw conclusions and then test their veracity.

It is true in very many cases, as C.A. Moser said: "The purpose of many surveys is simply to provide someone with an information. That someone may be a government department or a private body wanting to certain information for effective operation."

A careful analysis of history will reveal that social surveys are practically as old as the human race itself because from time immemorial the surveying of the various aspects of the groups, society and kingdoms was very much in vogue for administration. The ever-growing, socio-economic and other problems in human society instigated the social scientists to engage in the study of those problems and to find the causes and to take remedial measures. A good number of economists, sociologists, anthropologists, social reformers and social scientists have conducted a number of different types of surveys either independently or in collaboration with governments or research institutions. Those include general, specific and census survey technique to gather materials in a systematic way right from the ancient days.

The survey method is generally undertaken in almost all branches of knowledge for the following definite purposes:

(i) To investigate the present status of the various phenomena;

(ii) To simplify a survey already undertaken;

(iii) To find out the solution for unsolved problems;

(iv) To arrive at better methods for efficient administration;

(v) To obtain responses and reactions from large number of individuals; and

(vi) To gather a relatively large number of cases at a particular time.

The survey method has its own credibility as a research medium for it is more realistic than the experimental. Its basic and preliminary structure upon which the essential and reliable structure may be built, its echoing of the generalised voices of the individuals at large, its valid and accurate results and its interpretative facts and figures make it more so.

Glady suggests the following steps in the survey method: studying the situation and problem; formulating purposes; considering the type, scope and nature; securing cooperation; selecting the participating personnel; finding sources of data; preparing the survey report; estimating the effectiveness.

The methodology of the survey research involves various steps which may lead an investigator to unforeseen practical problems such as sampling, the validity of the instrument or techniques used to gather data, the validity of the questionnaire and the reliability of the data gathered from the respondents, etc.

The researcher should be alert and careful not to commit errors or blunders in the steps such as ascertaining the general objectives, specific objectives, sample, questionnaires, field work, processing and analysis of data and interpretation of the findings, to arrive at appreciably better findings.

The various types of survey and the different

techniques used in survey have their respective significance and value. In general, it may be said 'that the survey throws light on the various aspects of the social problems and helps in the understanding the causes of the problems and the mutual interplay of the causes.

A specialised survey may be called a depth survey because it studies a particular problem in a limited range. The conclusions of a specialised survey are much more reliable than those of general or widespread surveys. Accordingly, the specialised survey is more important from the scientific point of view. The postal survey is less expensive than the personal survey but it is possible only when all the respondents are literate. Moreover, in case of doubt in the respondent's mind the postal survey fails whereas the personal survey is undoubtedly reliable and therefore desirable.

The value of a primary survey is directly dependent upon the technique used. Hence, there is lack of comparative material which proves a stumbling block. However, the primary survey is highly important because through it a first hand attempt is made to gather well-organised information on a subject which proves to be a stepping stone for repetitive surveys. The census and income data can be kept reliable only through regular surveys.

Survey research has a wide scope. A great deal of information can be obtained from a large population. While surveys tend to be more expensive than laboratory and field experiments and field studies for the amount and quality of information they yield, they are economical. Survey research information is accurate within the sampling error ranges in the case of sporting activities.

5

TESTS AND MEASUREMENTS IN PHYSICAL EDUCATION

Like other subjects, successful teaching-learning of physical education also requires that the students should be tested and their achievements should be measured. Right from the outset of physical education programme the physical ability and fitness of the students are measured to ascertain as to what physical activities are suitable to them. After the completion of the programme they are again tested to ascertain how far they have developed their abilities. Hence test and measurement is the integral part of physical education. No programme can give out the desired results unless its implementation is well supervised and its ultimate outcomes are evaluated. Evaluation in physical education is done through the process of measurement.

MAIN AIMS OF TESTING AND MEASUREMENT

Main aims of testing and measurement in physical education are as under:

1. This is a means to ascertain how far the aims and objectives of physical education have been achieved.

2. It helps the physical instructor to detect drawbacks in his teaching. Improvement in instruction is not

possible without testing and measurement.

3. It helps in making the future programmes in a better way. Through evaluation the planners become aware of flaws in their previous plan and try to remove those flaws while planning the future programmes.

4. It helps the students to increase their knowledge. This is an important motivational force which motivates the students to gain more and more knowledge in physical education.

5. It helps in the classification of students. It is not possible to assess different abilities of an individual without evaluating his traits. On the basis of that assessment he is placed in a particular group, most suitable to him.

6. It helps the teacher in understanding the individual problem and weaknesses of each student and he can adjust his teaching accordingly.

7. It increases students interest in physical education. Every student is curious about his achievement. He always tries to know his progress in relation to his fellow students. He also tries to compare his performance with his previous performance and puts in more efforts to achieve better results.

8. It also helps in detecting an I removing physical defects of the students.

9. It makes teaching of physical education a meaningful and purposeful activity. It makes the students feel that participation in physical activities is not mere a past-time, but it has a certain purpose behind it.

10. Test and measurement is a basic tool for research in physical education.

CHARACTERISTICS OF A GOOD TEST

The characteristics of a good test are as under:

1. Reliability; 2. Validity;
3. Objectivity; 4. Practicability;
5. Comprehensiveness; 6. Economical;
7. Interesting; 8. A definite procedure;
9. Easy to score.

1. Reliability

Test should be reliable. Reliability of a teat means that whenever it is repeated under the same conditions, the response should approximately be the same. On the re-administration of the test under the same condition if the student gets approximately the same score, the test can safely be said as reliable.

2. Validity

A test is designed to measure a particular quality or trait. If it is successful in measuring that quality or trait, it will be considered valid. A strength-test will be considered to be valid if it correctly measures the strength of the students. Without validity the test will be good-for-nothing.

3. Objectivity

Objectivity means that personal influence of the tester should not involve in testing the achievements of the students. The personal likes and dislikes of the tester should not interfere with the results. If a test is administered by two different persons to the same student under the same conditions and the results remain similar, the test will be called objective. Objectivity ensures correct measurement of students.

4. Practicability

Test should be practicable The questions asked in a test should be intelligible and environment should be tension-free. Physical education is a practical activity. Hence practicability is a very significant quality of test designed for physical education.

5. Comprehensiveness

Test should be adequately comprehensive. This means that it should be vast enough to assess maximum aspects of one's ability. The more a test is comprehensive, the more will be his stability and reliability.

6. Economical

A good test should be economical. It should not involve much money and time.

7. Interesting

One reason of students' aversion to tests is their dull and dry nature. Most of the tests are designed and conducted in a dull way. As a result the students don't take interest in them. All the tests should be made interesting and the behaviour of testers towards the students should be sympathetic and encouraging. Test and measurement in physical education should particularly be made interesting. This should always be kept in mind that entertainment is one of the aims of physical education. Dull and dry testing will kill this aim of physical education., The students willingly prepare for the test when they are sure that it will be pleasant and interesting. An interesting test facilitates the right assessment of students.

8. A definite procedure

The procedure of test and measurement should be pre-determined. It should be definite as to what procedure will be adopted while testing and measuring different abilities of the students. A definite procedure facilitates the smooth conduct of test ad eaves lot of time and energy.

9. Easy to score

Test and measurement in physical education should be designed and conducted in-such a way that its scoring should not be difficult. Easy scoring will help in tabulation of result as early as possible. It will also ensure objective and judicious evaluation.

TYPES OF TESTS

For the measurement of different abilities of students several types of tests are designed— such as Intelligent Test, Aptitude Test, Psychological Test, Knowledge Test, Physical Efficiency Test, Achievement Test, Medical Test, Sports Skill Test etc.

No doubt all these different tests have some importance in physical education, but chiefly those tests are adopted in it through which the speed, agility, endurance, neuro-muscular co-ordination, sports-skill etc. of the students could be measured. From this point of view the following tests are used in physical education.

1. Medical Test

Through this test the health of the students is examined. This shows how far a student is healthy. Through this test the physical defects in the students are given proper treatments to remove those defects. Medical test is the necessary basis for the classification of students. So it should be given an important place, particularly, in the field of physical education. In the beginning of the session every student should be medically examined and his proper record should be maintained. Every student should be medically examined at least once a year and there should be adequate provision for the treatment and follow-up.

2. Anthropometric Test

Anthropometric test is an essential part of medical test. Through this test physical s stems of a student are examined-his height, chest, weight, development of muscles, strength of lungs, standing posture, sitting posture, walking posture etc., are measured and tested.

3. Physical Efficiency Test

Development of physical efficiency of students is one of the chief aims of physical education. To achieve this aim physical efficiency tests are conducted. Through these tests strength, speed, agility and endurance of the students is measured, It was in 1959 that, Government of India started physical efficiency movement for the benefit of the people of India. This movement is doing remarkable job in the development of physical efficiency of people.

Different physical activities are included in physical efficiency tests to measure different abilities of the students. For measuring the strength of the students 'Push-up' activity is included. Similarly, to measure the 'speed' of the students different types of races-as 50 Metre Race, 100 Metre Race etc.-are included. For the measurement of agility 'Long Jump' and 'High Jump' are included. Endurance ability is measured by long race.

4. Achievement Test

The skill of different activities achieved by the students is measured by Achievement Test. This type of test is very important in physical education because it helps in ascertaining as to how far the students have succeeded in achieving the skill involved in different activities.

HISTORY OF TESTS AND MEASUREMENTS

Testing and measuring is by no means a recent innovation in the program of physical education. Hitchcock, at Amherst, starting in 1861, and Sargent, at Harvard, beginning in 1880, were pioneers in the use of anthropometric measurements as applied to a physical development program. Sargent was also instrumental, in common with a number of other physical educators of his time, in developing the widespread popularity of strength tests during the period from approximately 1880 until around 1900. The intercollegiate strength test which was developed by Sargent and his group has been somewhat revised, first by F. R. Rogers, and second by McCloy, and in its new from is used extensively in the present-day program of physical education. Advances in knowledge concerning the physiology of the heart and circulation brought a change in emphasis from pure muscle building to improvement in physiological functioning and in all round physical condition; and with this change in viewpoint came an emphasis on cardiovascular tests.

These tests, however, failed to strike the fancy of the physical educators of that period, and although several types of such tests were developed, few have been widely used. At about the turn of the century, various types of physical ability tests began to receive widespread attention. The most popular of these consisted various combinations of the track and field type of events, and such tests have continued to grow in popularity.

Other types of ability tests, largely because they did not seem to be too directly connected with program needs to because they lacked objectivity, failed to arouse enough enthusiasm to cause them to be extensively used. These earlier testing programs, because of the strenuous nature of the physical activity programs which they encouraged, were largely restricted to the colleges and universities. Not until about 1908, when the Cleveland and New York public school systems organized their athletic leagues, was there any well-organized attempt at testing public school children. In 1913, the Playground and Recreation Association of America published the Athletic Badge Test for Boys.

This marked the first concerted effort at testing physical ability of public school children on a nation-wide scale. Tests of this type, however, had been in use for some years in a number of playgrounds and school systems. During the next few years most of the larger school systems introduced some testing and measuring programs into their physical education curricula. The Detroit and the California Decathlon Tests were notable examples of early testing programs which have, with some slight modifications, retained their popularity, and they may safely be used today as models to be followed in setting up similar programs. The brief history of early testing in this country, which has just been reviewed, should convey to the reader the attitude of the pioneer leaders in physical education toward testing and measuring in this field.

A vast majority of the physical educators today do not share this enthusiasm for testing and are prone to resist attempts to set up such programs. Their chief criticisms are that many of the available tests are neither reliable nor valid and that a testing program to meet their needs would involve too much time and, in many cases, too much expense. These criticisms are rapidly being overcome through the progress that has been made in the improvement of tests for physical education.

Reliable and valid tests of various skills, abilities, and capacities are now available. One or two weeks at the most should suffice for testing every boy and girl in school, and this, in connection with the increased time allotment for physical education which is becoming more prevalent, would enable the physical educator to improve vastly his physical education program.

A KNOWLEDGE TEST OF SPORTS

This test is presented as a means of stimulating interest, and testing knowledge, in the realm of sports. It is not assumed that it is worthwhile for a coach or a physical educator to become a walking sports-page summary, but, rather, that one is benefited by being conversant with certain aspects of sports in general. As a matter of fact, too high a score on this test may bespeak a waste of some of the precious hours of youth. By the same token, a very low score may disclose an appalling lack of interest in one of the most prominent topics of conversation in America today. This test requires 200 answers dealing with names of sports places, trophies, performers, terms, and "titles."

It purports to present a sampling of each, rather than a complete list of all phases concerned. This is not a standardized test. However, indications, based on scores made by majors in physical education classes, are that a score of 180 is excellent and a score of 100 or less is very poor.

TESTING FOR A PURPOSE

Tests and measurements are useful only if they help the teacher to do a better piece of work. Consequently, except for the use of tests for research purposes, testing should be limited to those tests which are to be used to achieve a definite educational purpose. The custom in the past has too often been to test every pupil in a haphazard manner, then to file the scores away without more than a cursory examination of them. This wasteful procedure has been one cause for condemning the use of tests generally. It stamps the entire program as lacking in educational values and unworthy of professional respect.

The instructor, in fear of being accused of laziness, incompetence, or of not "being progressive," puts on a show of testing for the benefit of his administrative superior—and then neglects to utilize the results. It is no wonder that many physical educators regard such testing as unnecessary and that many educational administrators question the validity of physical education programs. One of the more common errors in interpreting test results in that of expecting a test to give information for which it was not designed. This error is a natural outcome or lack of purpose as well as of ignorance of the broad field which testing covers at the present time.

Misinterpretation of tests may be worse than not testing at all; consequently, it behooves the tester to make a careful selection of his tests, to keep in mind the purpose, or purposes, for which each test is to be utilized, and to keep in mind the inherent nature of each test. Very briefly, the entire testing program should be planned with one or more of the following purposes in mind: classification of students, guidance, grading, motivation, measuring progress toward objectives, and research. We shall discuss each of these purposes in turn.

MOTIVATION

Most educators hold the opinion that testing and measuring are worthwhile if they have no other purpose than that of creating a greater interest in the activity program. Many self-testing devices of a stunt nature as well as the tests mentioned being made and his or her status relative to the group. If the group is a fairly homogeneous one, this will serve to motivate the vast majority of the pupils. Such increased incentives tend to raise the general level of class performance, and if, further, the grading is upon the basis of grades relative to general motor capacity, even the lower 5 or 10 per cent of the group may be encouraged and strongly motivated in spite of the fact that they will still be at the bottom of the group.

Incidentally, it is found that with good teaching, those who are, at the beginning, at the low end of a probability distribution improve very much more than those near the mean and still more than those near the top. In other words, the spread of the distribution will be greatly narrowed toward the high end. The curve becomes narrower but higher. This is a desirable outcome of both testing and teaching.

GRADING

The complexity of grading methods are treated more fully elsewhere in this text, and further mention of the educational value of scientific grading may seem repetitions; however, the problem is closely related to the testing program, and its final solution must be based in part upon a sound selection of tests. In this connection in physical education, it is possible to give grades based partly upon ability relative to capacity. The correlation between tests of general motor capacity and achievement test scores is high. This would be somewhat comparable to giving grades in classroom subjects in relation to the intelligence quotient or mental age.

In school work, this is frequently not feasible. For example, one would not wish to graduate a physician from a college of medicine and license him to practice simply because he had done wonderfully we for a moron. One would not wish to have his legal practice turned over to an individual who had been graduated from law school because he had done excellent work for an individual with an I.Q. of 80. In these fields, absolute grades seem to be the most desirable. In the field of physical abilities, it may be preferable to grade the individual relative to his capacity. Thus, he is encouraged by being given full recognition for how hard he tries.

This, of course, is not in accord with the not unusual practice of requiring the scores to be distributed according to the normal curve. If, however, justice to the pupil would indicate the desirability of the departure from the academic worship of the binominal curve, it would seem the part of wisdom to so depart. In physical education testing, it is frequently feasible "to announce the examination question in advance." To give out the examination questions in arithmetic a semester before the individual was to take the examination would probably result in everyone's getting—though not necessarily deserving—an A.

To announce that the all-around score in four track and field events—naming the events—will be used as one of the term examinations does not insure that every one of the pupils will break the world's records in these events. To announce the twenty apparatus or tumbling stunts which will be used as an examination at the end of the learning period does not insure that everyone will have passed all of those tests. It does, however, give direction to the practice and give each individual an opportunity to know what his goals are to be. This type of objective testing offers possibilities in the area of physical education which are not readily achievable in the area of the classroom studies.

GUIDANCE

The average physical educator is often at a loss to explain or to prescribe corrective measures for the shortcomings of his poorer pupils. To prescribe a program of activity which will most effectively bring about rapid improvement requires a definite knowledge of handicaps, limitations, and weaknesses. This knowledge can be obtained only through a well-planned testing program intended to give a profile of individual strengths and weaknesses. To illustrate how such a profile can be obtained from the scores recorded, let us illustrate from the tests mentioned above under the heading of the General Motor Capacity Score.

We will set up an hypothetical situation in which test scores might aid in guiding the teacher to aid his pupils. In addition to computing the General Motor Capacity Score, each of the first three test items may be assessed in terms of what is usually called a T-score. The T-score is much like a standard score but is usually computed from percentiles, assuming a normal distribution of ability, but not of the test scores. In this case, 50 will represent the average score, 60 will represent one standard deviation above the average score, 70 two standard deviations above the average score, and so forth. Forty represents one standard deviation below the average score, 30 two standard deviations below the average score, and so on.

Classification of students into homogeneous groups

Many differences exist between activity programs in physical education and in other educational fields. The chief difference, and perhaps the most fundamental, is the difference in social relationships. Learning in many of the academic subjects is more or less a subjective, individual affair. In physical education, however, the learning process is an overt one, and the results are reading apparent to all fellow students.

The boy or girl who constantly falls behind his group in performance is apt to be regarded as inferior by them, and the individuals who are far superior to their groups tend to feel that there is little challenge to their abilities.

The student's attitude toward the whole program is frequently influenced by the degree to which he is placed in a group of those of approximately his own performance level. The solution to this problem lies in a homogeneous grouping of the entire student body on the basis of sex, size, maturity, strength, speed, and skill. The simplest approach to this problem of homogeneous grouping is grouping based on sex, age, height, and weight, McCloy and Cozens and his co-workers have worked independently for the past twenty years on this problem and have obtained almost identical results.

This type of grouping, to which McCloy has given the name of The Classification Index, is more applicable to boys than to girls. McCloy gives no norms for girls in this type of index, but Cozens and his associates have given such norms, though the correlations between the index and the performance for girls are low. This type of index does not take into account strength, speed, or skill. It is, however, a very easy and convenient way to classify students. A much more accurate method of classification is that given by McCloy's test of general motor capacity.

This test is made up of the Sargent jump, the ten-second squat thrust, the Iowa brace Test, and the Classification Index. This test battery tends to give a composite measure of speed of muscular contraction, of agility, and of an all-round type of motor educability, in addition to the measurement of size and maturity offered by the Classification Index. This test results in a General Motor Capacity Score which is comparable to mental age in intelligence testing, or to a total intelligence test score.

The test score can be turned into the Motor Quotient, which is comparable to the intelligence quotient in the intellectual field, by dividing 100 times the General Motor Capacity Score by the norm for the Classification Index in boys or the norm for age in girls. In addition to this total test score, the individual items can be further analyzed. This, however, will be discussed below under the heading of guidance. A somewhat simpler test for classification is the Physical Efficiency Index, which is composed of the standing broad jump, a shot-put from a stand, and weight. These three scores, when properly combined, correlate very highly indeed with the individual's ability to perform.

The test does not tell as much or give as many facets of the individual's physical capacity as does the General Motor Capacity Score or the Motor Quotient, but it can be administered very rapidly and correlates very highly with performance in other skills.

MEASURING PROGRESS TOWARD ACCOMPLISHMENT OF OBJECTIVES

Educational progress is best made by first clearly defining the objectives toward which the educational process should point. Then the educator should set up the educational processes designed to achieve those objectives. Third, he should attempt to measure pupil achievement to see whether or not his educational procedures have been successful. In the field of physical education, the tests lend themselves especially well to this end. Hence, one of the most important uses of tests is to measure progress toward the objectives. The objectives are as follows:

1. Physical objectives. The measurement of the

accomplishment of physical objectives might well be classified somewhat as follows:

(a) Tests of achievement in posture and body mechanics generally. Part of these tests will be objective or semiobjective tests of posture, or position of feet; part will be the more subjective estimates of body mechanics such as are employed in the ordinary orthopedic diagnosis.

(b) Measurement of improvement in circulo-respiratory endurance. Such tests activities as the Carlson Test or tests of running endurance, particularly when equated against the speed of the individual, are excellent for this purpose.

(c) Measurement of improvement in muscular endurance. Tests such as chinning, push-ups, sit-ups, full squats or squat jumps, and activities of that type lend themselves to measurement in this area.

(d) Appraisal of nutritional status. In the larger sense of the team, this is a very difficult thing to accomplish. In the narrower sense, however, of the appraisal of weight relative to normal weight, of the amount of subcutaneous fat, and of general muscular development, this is relatively easy. Such measurements can be made by use of modern anthropometric techniques.

2. Test of knowledge. This category of tests is represented by the objective paper and pencil tests and may be used to measure progress in knowledge of rules, of techniques, and of health principles generally.

3. Improvement in general ability to develop power, as represented by the type of activities usually known as "racial activities." These are activities like running,

jumping, throwing, climbing, and vaulting, and represent improvement in the use of the physical machine up to the limits of the individual's general motor capacity. In this area, the track and field type of tests assumes an importance out of proportion to the general importance of track and field activities generally. In all power events, an increase in strength will improve the time, distance or height of the performance.

4. Measurement of improvement in characteristics usually associated with improvement in character and personality. This type of measurement is represented by ratings of character or personality qualities and is based upon comprehensive studies of how best to assess these qualities accurately.

5. Measurement of improvement in skills. One of the important objectives of physical education is to master skills of sports activities, of games and athletics, and, especially, to develop the various components of skill, such as accuracy, balance and muscular control generally. Here, the achievement tests and the tests of accuracy and balance bulk large.

USE OF TEST FOR RESEARCH

The foundation for progress in any science or any educational field is research. The tests mentioned in this chapter are the results of research labours by men and women who have devoted much time to these problems. Research represents the advanced stage of study in any profession; and, consequently, many years of training and experience are required before one can safely attempt to use the techniques of research for the solution of problems involving the improvement of testing and measuring methods.

The more advanced students who intend to enter the field of research, however, should become acquainted with the various techniques of research which apply to testing and to the development of tests. To the student not interested in doing research, knowledge of the techniques of research used will enable him to evaluate new tests as they appear in the literature. Physical educators untrained in such research methods should not attempt to devise standard tests; instead to competent research workers in the field of testing and physical education should fall the task of producing valid and reliable tests.

To do this well requires years of training in testing techniques plus a background of advanced statistical methods. The average physical educator should, therefore, be content to study and employ the testing techniques described and recommended by experts in this branch of physical education. For a description of the tests to be used, the student should refer to the standard textbook on tests and measurements.

TESTING AS AN EDUCATION PROCEDURE

Progressive physical educators agree that the education of every boy and girl is not complete without a systematic and well-organized program of physical and health education. It has been relatively easy to convince the well-trained, broad-minded educator that such a program is a necessity; but to convince him that present-day practices in physical education are educationally sound has not been as easy. The chief criticisms offered by the general educator are: (1) that physical activity programs are not well organized, and (2) that the testing and grading methods employed are not up to the standards of such testing devices for other subjects.

The latter criticism is largely occasioned by the failure of the physical educator to plan his testing program purposefully and to use the results to improve, motivate, and evaluate the results of his program in terms of his objectives. Until testing programs are more intelligently conceived, carried out, and interpreted, they will not be considered as important adjuncts to the general educational program.

Fundamental Concepts of testing. Before any teacher can serve his pupils to the best advantage, it is quite obvious that he must study each individual in terms of his or her innate capacities and present abilities. All tests are designed to measure one or other of these two factors; the vast majority are tests of general ability or of specific skills or knowledge. Tests of intelligence and aptitude are especially valuable to the classroom teacher in that they furnish an index of what to expect from each individual in the classroom. Tests of general motor capacity are equally valuable to the teacher of physical education. Intelligent procedures in testing in physical education aim at measuring not only the pupil's present ability but his ability relative to his capacity.

This measurement of ability relative to capacity gives an index to the extent of his development; in other words, it tells how good or how poor the pupil is in proportion to what he should be able to do, and, as such, this type of test score is most valuable to the teacher in his efforts to serve the individual. The importance of test interpretation is illustrated by the queries of the serious-minded pupils who, before attempting a chinning test, will ask specifically, "How many times should I be able to chin myself?" or, having been told that he had jumped a certain number of centimeters in the Sargent jump, asks, "How good is that?" or "What is a good jump?" Questions such as these are indicative of pupil interest in testing, and if this attitude upon the part of the pupil is to be maintained, it is important that the tester be able to give him intelligent answers on the sport.

This requires the use of tests for which norms or standards are available, and these norms should be kept where they can readily be refereed to when they are needed to answer questions by pupils. Another method is to post the standards where the students can read the answers. It is unfair to expect all students to achieve equal performances in any type of physical capacity or ability tests, because some may be labouring under server handicaps, and others may have distinct advantages. Such factors as physique, training, agility, strength, and various sensory or neuromuscular co-ordination should be considered in interpreting deviations from the norms for such tests.

In strength testing, size and maturity must be considered; in testing sport skills, innate physical capacity, previous training, and physical disabilities should be taken into consideration. In attempting to measure nutritional status, not only should age, sex, height, and weight be taken into consideration, but other measures which determine body build, the amount of fat on the body, muscular development, and so forth should be considered. Such knowledge of significant elements in vital to the intelligent interpretation of the test results and the tester should always keep this concept uppermost in his mind when passing judgment on his students. Another concept which is well known but still merits some discussion is that of measuring improvement.

Progress is the aim of all education, and appreciation of progress provides the incentive for both pupil and teacher to carry on. In physical education progress is specific activities can be measured quite objectively and the pupil often feels real satisfaction because this improvement is do easily recognized. Increased speed in running and increased distance in jumping and throwing can be readily measured. Increases in the number of times that one can "Chin" or do push-ups or sit-ups can be readily counted, and they are important in assessing the individual's physical condition. An important point that is often overlooked is that equal amounts of increase at different levels of ability are not necessarily indicative of equal amounts of improvements or progress.

For example, to increase one's speed in the 100-yard dash from 11 seconds to 10.8 seconds is not so great an achievement as increasing one's speed from 10 seconds to 9-8 seconds. Overlooking this simple concept offers a grave injustice to the more advanced pupil and causes the teacher to ministerpret the significance of the improvement. MCCloy studied the principle underlying such unequal increment of point values, particularly as related to track and field event. These increments seem to be dependent upon the amount of power developed relative to the weight of the individual. In general in the track and field type of events the amount of increment in points increases as the level of performance increases.

6

BIOLOGICAL BASIS OF PHYSICAL EDUCATION

Concepts of Nature and Nurture

It has been customary for a long time to regard nature and nurture as mutually antagonistic and exclusive factors that determine the behaviour of individuals. The inheritance of traits and the effect of environment have provided the battleground for long and heated arguments. With the advance of genetics as a science of inheritance, the exclusive character of one influence or the other has been seriously challenged. Long accustomed to authoritarian views about nature, modern man retains in his beliefs, customs and speech notions about nature of an exceedingly bizarre character. These range from the doctrine of man's inheritance evil nature to the concept that nature is always right.

The study of genetics has afforded the basis for new interpretations of nature. The failures of man to build a good world are due neither to his inheritance evilness nor to his slavish devotion to and following of nature. On the contrary, the present incapacity to utilize constructively the forces of the environment and his own potential powers forms the problem.

Society rapidly changing under the force of man's invention, must now face the problem of human behaviour. Thus, the crucial tasks we confront in physical education are those of nurture rather than nature. We are learning slowly, but surely that to get a better world to live in, we must secure better living in the world rather than attempt to secure a transformation of nature.

The rejection of the idea that nature exerts an all-pervading influence in human life does not deny to nature a position of considerable importance. This influence, however, often relates to an earlier life of man. Man is still equipped by nature to live in an environment vastly different from the life that now is, as a result of science, art, reasoning, habit, language, tools, books, and various customs of his race. Hence, each new individual must unlearn much of his nature in order to live with others in the crowded co-ordinated life of industrial society.

By nature man cries from pain and fights for things he wants, he grabs and snatches from others. By nurture of particular kinds, he learns to merit what he takes, and to earn or deserve the satisfaction of his wants. The present understanding of nature rejects the notion that nature is always right or always wrong or half and half. It recognizes that the individual possess drives, urges and impulses to certain kinds of behaviour and that these should be strengthened at times, weakened at times, and completely checked at times.

Physical education in the selection of activities should recognize that man is prepared by nature to engage in certain kinds of activity. Many of the persistent problems in physical education today are clarified by reference to the facts of nature. The fact that man presents in the racial patterns of his nervous system certain underlying predispositions to function in well-defined motor activities characterized in type and quality by his motor experiences over thousands of years, that he is urged on by his very nature to exploit these established organizations, and that, under proper guidance, such expressions may be made to serve high causes and noble ends is of outstanding import.

Nature proclivities of man represent enormous changes from original traits. Learning and nurture in its various forms are represented in the liking of boys for fishing, sport and adventure since nature knows nothing of sport records. Nature's tendencies may go as far as to enjoy throwing a small object and swinging a club like thing, but the majority of the sports of youth are modifications and adaptation of these early proclivities. Such modifications are natural activities in their basic patterns, but all reflect the influence of nurture.

Today, biological and cultural evolutions have far reaching implications. In ancient days, it was required for the existence of man to indulge in various kinds of physical activities. Now, it is necessary for human beings to keep them fit to sustain their biological posture proper. Physical activities are practised to keep an individual emotionally and mentally fit. An inheritance of structure and function has been brought by biological evolution which has aroused requirement of care and attention. Modern age is age of technology and this kind of living has affected to physiques of general people to a lot of extent. Not only this, they have brought various negative effect on the mental abilities of people. One should remember that a sound mind can only reside in a sound body.

Meanings of Growth and Development

Generally word growth and development are used synonymously, however, there is a difference in the meanings of these concepts. Technically, growth of an individual means increase in mass, while development is the organization of that tissue into functional units or powers. Development of the child can be judged in part by growth, but growth may occur without a corresponding development.

Nutrition and various hygienic factors condition growth and development. While physical education influences growth, its chief interest is in development.

Growth

The process through which body increases in size and shape is known as growth. Process of growth is biological in nature. An increase in mass is termed as growth. From the first growth of the fertilized ovum until maturity of the individual is reached numerous forces determine growth. Some organs evens continue to grow in old age also. Thus, a quantitative increase in the size and shape of the body is termed as growth. When these organs changes in size and shape, it is known as physical growth. All the organs of body grow at different rate. For this reason, growth is considered a tangible biological process. In this process, various organs of the human body develop in respect of size, height and weight. There occurs an increase in the size of cells of body and muscles. In body structure, various kinds of changes take place and these changes are of quantitative nature.

Development

A process which brings human body towards the point of maturity is known development. In other words, process of development is concerned with advancement of human body. The various kinds of qualitative changes that takes place in human body are considered development in true sense.

Process of development is more concerned with external factors. If all these external factors are not ensured properly, development will not take place properly. It can be said that the process under which capabilities of an individual get expanded which provide him with greater facility in functioning is known as development.

Although concepts of development and growth are different, but they are inter-related to each other. Growth is a means to achieve development. For the development of functional capacities of human beings, growth functions as a basis. At no stage, it is possible to acquire proper development with improper growth. Development of an individual is concerned with his mental, intellectual and social aspects. Development process consists of acquisition of skills and knowledge of various fields.

Thus it can be said that both the processes of growth and development are complimentary to each other and it is not possible to achieve one successfully without achieving another. Development is a life long procedure while growth is a limited period process. An human being grow upto a certain age or period in his life but process of development continues throughout the lifetime.

Learning

When an individual acquires knowledge of some skill, he is said to have learnt that skill. Learning can be of different kinds and every kind of learning brings about a kind of change in the behaviour of individuals.

With the process of growth, a child's body becomes more heavier and taller. With the result of development, capacities of human body increases and organs of body become more capable to understand various kinds of complex functions. As an individual becomes maturer, his systems become more adapted to handle various kinds of situations. As a result of an individual's interaction with the environment, he continues to learn. All these processes are not fully independent in nature, but they are inter-related to each other in one way and other.

Maturation

Maturation is a physiological development that occur in human body from time to time. This kind of development is qualitative in nature. This process occurs as a result of biological functions.

In development of a child, various processes play important roles. These processes are growth, maturation and learning. These are related to each other and function properly in association with each other.

Kinds of Development

As development is a life long process, it can be in different forms. There are three kinds of developments which take place in an individual, which are :—

a. Social Development,

b. Motor Development,

c. Mental Development.

Social Development : The process which helps in developing the qualities of human behaviour is known as social development. These qualities include quality of working in co-operation and co-ordiation with others and quality to lead other persons.

Motor Development : Development of general body control, fine motor skills and large muscle movements are considered part of this kind of development. Such developments take place with the help of movements like running, jumping and throwing.

Mental Development : With the increase in age, mental abilities of an individual also increases. Such type of increase in mental capabilities of human beings is known as mental development. With such kind of development, an individual becomes able to distinguish between different kind of things, learning difficult skills or things, and gets reasoning ability.

Thus on the basis of above discuss it can be said that there lies a difference between growth and development. The points of differences that exist between these concepts are as follows :—

a. One can see the process of growth in an individual, however, it is not possible to see the process of development.

b. It is possible to measure growth in physical terms, but it is not possible to measure development in such terms.

c. Growth is such a process which lasts only for a limited time. After a certain age, process of growth ceases to take place, however, development is a long process, which lasts throughout the life time. Right from the time a child takes birth in the world upto the time he dies, process of development goes on.

d. Heredity of an individual plays an important role in defining the limits of growth, while external factors affect process of development to a lot of extent.

Fundamental Principles of Growth and Development

Both the processes of growth and development are guided by certain fundamental principles. These principles should be kept in mind while formulating the physical education programmes. Some of the important principles of growth and development are as follows :—

a. It is with the interaction of heredity and environment that processes of growth and development take place.

b. A specific genetic sequence is being followed by processes by growth and development. The nature of these processes do not remain same at different stages. They become complex from simple state with span of time.

c. Process of growth and development are long term procedures. They are gradual in nature. These are co-related with the life span of an individual. Long the life span of an individual, long will be these processes.

d. Growth and development processes are creative in nature. As a result of these processes, various kinds of changes take place in functional and behavioural features of the individual.

e. Quality of germs and other external factors affect these processes to a lot of extent.

f. Rate of increase of both these processes varies from each other. In each individual, these processes take place with different pace.

Factors that Affect Processes of Growth and Development

Processes of growth and development can be affected by various factors, some of which are : Environmental Factors, Genetic Factors, Nutritional Factors and Physical Education Programmes.

All these factors affect growth and development in different manners, which has been discussed in the following manner :—

Effect of Environmental Factors on Growth and Development

It is firstly very necessary to understand what factors are included in the specific category of environmental factors. Factors like healthy traditions, geographical conditions, education, health related facilities, and social codes are some of the important components of this category.

Effect of Genetic Factors on Growth and Development

That branch of biology which deals with the heredity is known as Genetics. In all the human bodies, some genes are present which help in passing some characteristics of parents to the children. Patterns of growth from one generation to another are being controlled by genes, because of which they are considered the most powerful of living forces. The fundamental traits which are being transferred from parents to children are height, speed, agility etc. If the genes of the parents are weak, then child can be affected by various diseases or some diseases which parents faces, can be faced by their children also.

Effect of Nutritional Factors on Growth and Development

To its optimum limits, well balanced diet, climatic conditions and stages of growth and development affect pace of the processes of growth and development to a lot of extent.

Effect of Physical Education Programme on Growth and Development

While designing the physical education programme for school and college children, their needs and requirements should be kept in mind. If their needs will be ignored while designing such programme, no positive results can be obtained, otherwise, possibilities of getting negative results will arise.

It is believed by experts that all the teachers or physical educators should have thorough knowledge of each and every aspect relating to growth and development. Now the question arises that why it is necessary for all the teachers to have such knowledge. A teacher imparts knowledge to a large number of students and these students differ from each other in various respects. All they belong to different socio-economic backgrounds, environments, caste and have different genders. Because of difference in all these factors, there arises a lot of difference between all the children. In their level of education, these factors play an important role.

The basic aim of each and every teacher is to impart education to students. It is well known that there are some qualities already present in all the students, which are being explored by teacher in such a way that students can learn the things easily. No teacher can exploit such qualities unless and until he has thorough knowledge about the qualities different students possess. It is very necessary for him to have a thorough knowledge of fundamental principles of growth and development. As a student passes through different age groups, various kinds of characteristics emerge because of all these factors. Teacher should have proper knowledge about these kind of different characteristics. He should have thorough knowledge of factors which affect the processes of growth and development.

Students are considered to be a treasure for a nation and a teacher plays an important role in bringing desirable changes in the behaviour of children. In this way, teachers create good and responsible citizens for the nation in an indirect way. They play an important role in the process of national development. Not only this, if teacher has the knowledge of various aspects of growth and development, he can without any problems, understand the students in terms of their past and can predict their future in advance.

Influence of Heredity and Environmental Factors on Processes of Growth and Development

Various biological and psychological factors affect the heredity and environment of an individual. Different opinions are being provided by different experts. Experts who believe in biological scientists advocate in favour of various inherited qualities for an integral development of a student. According to such experts, personality of an individual do not change and they remain as they are however, behaviour of students or any individual can get change because of the various persons they come into contact with. When the question of all around development of an individual arises, importance of certain innate qualities cannot be ignored. Qualities of aggression, self-preservation are such kinds of innate qualities. Such qualities are inherited biologically and thcy affect an individual's personality to a lot of extent.

If viewed according to this aspect, it will realise that utmost importance is being provided to inherited traits and environmental factors have been ignored to a lot of extent. There are some experts who criticise this concept on this basis. Such experts do not accept the superiority of inherited traits in comparison to environmental factors. Such experts are firm believers of the notion that it is not possible to create any player, but players are born with such qualities which help them in becoming outstanding players. Quality and performance of players can be only improved with the help of various services, like diet controls and proper motivation.

After analysing both the arguments, it will be realised that an extreme approach in favour of heredity and environment has been adopted by both kinds of experts. On the basis of both kinds of arguments, it can be said that heredity and environment plays an important role in shaping the personality of an individual, thus man is actually a produce of heredity and environment. Sports is a social institution and biological necessity, because of which a sportsman should be considered as an blend or mixture of the two. A sportsman get not affected only by biological factors but sociological forces also play an important role in affecting him. In addition to these, various other factors play a very important role in shaping the personality of an individual. Such factors include social practices, religious attitudes and type of school in which student gets education.

Today, the function of physical educator is not only concerned with imparting education relating to various activities to the students, but they also provide guidance to them in different kinds of personal matters.

Thus it can be said that it is not possible to bring any kind of change in the genetic make up of any individual, but it is possible to develop these inherited potentials to a lot of extent. This thing can be done by providing him a cordial environment in which he can easily and without any problem bring a kind of development in his inherited factors. It is in the very effective manner that factors of heredity and environment influence processes of growth and development.

Age and Sex Differences in Concern with Physical Activities and Sports

Today, in our country, we find that at various levels of education boys and girls get education simultaneously, and it is not possible to appoint separate physical educators for both kinds of students. Physical educators should kept in mind that boys and girls are different from each other in various respects. Various kinds of important differences are being found in the students of both the sexes.

Various kinds of differences take place after the stage of puberty. Upto the puberty stage, hardly any difference is seen between boys and girls but as they cross this stage, one can very clearly view the differences that emerge in them. While formulating physical education programme for the students of both sexes, physical educator should kept in his mind all these marked differences. These differences not only result because of various biological factors, but various social factors also play an important role in bringing such kind of differences. For this reason, physical educators should construct separate programmes for boys and girls, otherwise, it will not bring any kind of beneficial results.

Some kind of Differences in Males and Females

Some of the mark differences which are being found between a girl and boy are as follows :—

a. Rate of growth of the students of both the sexes is not same. They do not grow at the same pace. In the age of early adolescence, girls grow faster in comparison to boys but their rate of growth diminishes after the age of 14. In case of boys, they grow with a slow pace before the adolescence age, but their this rate diminishes after the age of 14 to 16 years.

b. After crossing the age of 14, girls students find it difficult to run faster without any problem the reason of which is that they have broader and shallow pelvis. In case of boys, this kind of problem does not arise because they have narrow pelvis in relation to girls and does not find it difficult to run at any rate.

c. Generally it is found that height of girls remain smaller or shorter in comparison to boys. They can attain height only in early age of maturity, but boys can attain height even in later stages of maturity.

d. Girls also find it difficult to jump properly because they have large body and shorter limbs, which makes their centre of gravity low. In comparison to girls, boys have shorter trunk and long legs. They have a high centre of gravity which provide them with an unstable position. Because of this reason, boys do not find any problem in jumping events.

e. Girls have smaller heart but a faster pulse rate. This is the main reason why the pulse rate of the girl players increases in the beginning of exercise, but slower down after the exercise. Because of more muscle tissues, boys have larger heart in comparison to girls and have better blood circulation because of which in the beginning of exercise, they do not get tired easily.

f. Girls cannot perform better than boys in the field of pulling and punching activities because they have less muscular strength. In comparison to them, boys have more muscular power and because of which they can perform activities of punching, kicking and putting better or efficiently.

g. Reaction and movement time of girls is very slow in comparison to boys.

h. One of an important change that can take place only in girls is the beginning of menstruation cycle. This cycle results because of biological activities. In boys, this kind of no such biological activity take place.

i. Girls use upper part of their chest to breath more shallowly while boys breaths deeply in comparison to girls.

All the differences mentioned above affect performances of girls and boys students to a lot of extent. Physical educator should have a thorough knowledge of all these differences. From the above discussion, one can easily predict that girls are being placed at an inferior position in comparison to boys because of various biological factors. Age and sex differences are the very important aspects, which a physical educator should kept in mind while preparing programmes for students of both the sexes.

Different Phases of Age

The process of growth do not take place with the same pace in different age groups. We find varying degree of changes or fluctuations in the rate of this process. In a school, a large number of students get education and they all differ in various respect from each other. A physical educator has to provide education or training to all the students with varying differences. Because of the differences in physical and mental abilities of students, it become a difficult task for the physical educator to provide education to all of them in the same manner and at the same place.

It is indicated by the processes of growth and development that a child gets developed through various stages and one can find various kinds of differences in all the stages. Various kinds of changes are being found in an infant and an adolescent. Various criterion can be used to classify the students into various groups. For classifying the students, it is not necessary to have proper knowledge of their age in terms of month and years. One can easily find required data from register of the school. In our country, some people do not get registration of the birth of their child because of which, sometimes the problem of identifying their age arises. In such kind of situations, the criteria that is used to classify the students is their developmental characteristics. All these kinds of developmental characteristics provide different kinds of age, which play an important role in determining the personality of a student.

Different kinds of age, which result from various developmental characteristics are as follows :—

a. Anatomical Age,

b. Chronological Age,

c. Mental Age, and

d. Physiological Age

Anatomical Age

The process which brings a kind of development in the skeletal system of an individual is known as anatomical age. In determining the anatomical age of a person, quality of bone structure plays an important role. To determine the extent or rate of development taking place in skeletal system, technique of X-ray is being used.

Skeletal development of a child is affected to a lot of extent by the kind of food he or she takes. Thus, the level of nutrition in the foods of child plays an important role in determining the rate of development of skeletal in an individual.

What kind of weight exercises should be practised by the different students, this important thing is determined by considering the anatomical age of the child. Some children have strong skeleton while some have soft. Children with soft skeleton should not be allowed to practice heavy exercises, as it can create various kinds of problems in their skeleton systems.

Chronological Age

Age of a person that is determined by the day on which he was born and the time of this occurrence. Thus that age of a person which can be recorded in terms of years, months and days is termed as chronological age. To calculate this kind of age, the day on which child takes birth and the day on which he dies are being taken into consideration.

Generally, this kind of age is being used to classifying

a students in various categories. To decide whether a student should be included in the junior, sub-junior or senior teams, this kind of age is considered.

The manner in which development in one student take place differ from other students. Various kinds of changes are being viewed in various individuals in terms of physical qualities because individual rate of growth of each individual differ from each other. It is because of difference in the rate of growth with leads a kind of difference in mental ability of different students. Generally, for classifying students into various categories, their chronological age is being taken into account.

Mental Age

To the mental development of a child, his mental age is concerned. Mental development can be considered a process of mental maturation taking place in an individual. One thing should be kept in mind that there lies a lot of difference between physical and mental maturity. There is generally no relationship between mental maturity and physical development. We can find various individuals who have grown up in terms of physique, but not have attained a developed state of brain.

Various kinds of psychological tests are being used to detect the mental age of students. If any student is physically developed, he should not be considered mentally mature. Some children becomes maturer in terms of their mental abilities earlier and some later. Mental age of students can be determined with the help of various psychological tests. By knowing the level of mental development of a student, a teacher can very easily and properly construct the kind of physical education programme that suits him. Age groups should be formed, the basis of which should be body structure of students, their standards and objectives. Principle of homogeneity should be followed in order to classify the students into different categories. Same technique or programme should not be designed for all the students because every student differ from each other in various respect. Children of different age group should be trained differently and competitions between students of different age groups should not be organised. If matching is done properly, it provides a kind of confidence to the students and chances of their becoming injured decreases to a lot of extent.

Physiological Age

Physiological capabilities of students affect their age to a lot of extent. Generally, it is concerned with puberty. While calculating the age of a child, secretion of hormones from various glands and functional conditions of the organs should be taken into account. In case of girls, this age can be calculated on the basis of set of menstruation cycles, while in case of boys, growth of hair in the armpit can be taken or considered the base.

If age of the students is known to the physical educator, it becomes easy for him to prepare work schedules for different students. Some students with advanced chronological age are found to be immature in terms of physiological terms. This is an important factor which obstructs the physical activity programme to a lot of extent. Physiological age of children should be taken into account while working out the activity loads for them. Only those activities should be practised or used which suit the physiological age of the students. Children, having similar physiological age should be provided training at the same time. Only those children should be allowed to play with each other who belong to same physiological age group.

Thus, there are various kinds of ages through which various children passes from. The age in years, months and days of a child may not compare with the age of his development. Anatomical or physiological items in the individual may run ahead or lag behind in development for the normal age. The ossification of bones indicates anatomical age. This may be determined by the x-ray. Physiological age represents a functional condition and in relation to chronological age, may present marked variation.

Chronological age is a poor measure of capacity in either boys or girls. Physiological maturity represented in sexual development may range over a period of four to five years. Maturity may come at 10½ years or not until 16½ years. The median age for this development is between 13½ and 14 years. Early maturity is not a sign of poor health. Tall girls mature generally earlier than short ones.

Physical education should take into account physiological age in conduct of activities. Physiological age has significance for physical education. Children tend to play with others of their same physiological age and they select activities suited to their stage of development. Girls are older physiologically than boys. Moreover, early or late maturity of youths may present adjustment problems of which the teacher should be aware. Large size in a girl often complicates the posture problem, and if the breasts are well developed, this sign of maturity may lead to a postural stoop and a marked decrease of interest in sports activities. Small size in a boy is likewise contrary to the ideals of the culture and may produce emotional problems of compensatory character.

Different Kinds of Bodies

Different biological, psychological, sociological, and cultural factors effect physical characteristics to a lot of extent and this fact result differences in varying degree in the body type of different individuals. From ancient times, it is believed that an individual's body type is related to various factors, such as his health, immunity for diseases and physical performance. Taking this thinking as a base, various experts have various body structures in different categories.

For all the individuals, it is very important to study the kind of physique. This concept is related to understanding of various concepts, like physical and mental state of the individual and his emotional condition. A physical educator have to provide education to different kinds of students, for this reason, he should have thorough knowledge relating to the physique pattern of all the students. With the help of such knowledge, he will be able to do his function of imparting knowledge to students very easily. Not only this, with the help of such knowledge, he can, without any problem, maintain discipline in the class and can classify the students into different categories.

Information relating to physique of undergraduate students of physical education should be get from their parents. It is believed by some experts that human beings differ from each other to such an extent that it is not possible to categorise them into two or three categories. According to these experts, human bodies are made up of some primary components, and to classify the body types into different categories, these components should be used as the base. Endomorph, Ectomorph and Mesomorph are these primary components which make up a human body.

Endomorph

This is one kind of body structure. People with such structure of body are able to digest the hard food, through which they get the energy. They have round heads, broad face and square jaw. Their abdomen is large in size. Size of their neck is generally short. They have fatty breasts. They have broad feet with low arch. Their skin is of hairy and thick type. Their buttocks are heavy in weight. They broad palms and their fingers are short in length.

Such kind of people over-estimate their abilities. They generally remains in relaxed and good mood. They get bore very easily from routine work. In various kinds of sports activities, such people take part.

Ectomorph

People with such body build have poor digestive system and have less energy output. Their body structure seems to be very delicate. They have small face and a sharp nose. Neck of such kind of people is quite slender and they have long arms. Buttocks and legs of such kind of people is quite thin. They have long feet. Their skin is soft and have a lots of hair. Their vital capacity is quite low, but they are tall. They do functions or various works with low speed.

Under-estimation of their abilities is an important feature of such kind of people. They are ambition, but lack self-confidence. They try to solve various kinds of problems at their mental level and make use of their energy to a limited extent. They feel irritated and tensed in very simple problems or conditions. The kind of sports activities in which they like to part includes : Basketball, Volleyball and Running.

Mesomorph

Such kind of people have medium height. They are generally considered athletic type persons. Their bones are large in size and prominent in nature. They have long face bones and their calvin bones are quite heavy. They have large abdomen and low waist. Their buttocks are heavy in weight and they have heavy fore legs. They have rough skin. In nature, they like to dominate others, are full of energy and like to task various kinds of risks in their life. They can make decisions very quickly and can handle difficult problems on their own. They have a direct forward nature and have a clear mind.

Thus, various kinds of body types are being classified into above mentioned categories, but it is not necessary that only these categories can provide authentic information about the bodily structure of an individual.

7

PHILOSOPHY OF PHYSICAL EDUCATION

The word physical refers to body, and indicates bodily characteristics such as strength, speed, endurance, flexibility, health coordination and performance. It seemingly contrasts the body with the mind. The term education when used in conjunction with physical, refers to a process of education that develops the human body especially fitness and movement skills. Therefore, it transcends all misconceptions and misgivings about physical education as a field of teaching and being considered as an ingredient of general education.

A bird's eye-view of various definitions of physical education is essential. Physical Education as understood is such a cultivation of power and capabilities of student as will enable him to maintain his bodily condition in the best working order providing at the same time for the greater efficiency of his intellectual and spiritual life. It is proclaimed that physical education should aim to improve the mass of students and to give them as much health, strength and stamina as possible to enable them to perform the duties that await them after they leave their college."

These early definitions, laid emphasis on (i) the development of physical qualities which enable the individual to live his life successfully and efficiently and (ii) the process which is essentially educational in perspective.

Physical Education is rightly recognized as an integral part of education. The existence of man is primarily physical. The first lessons a human child learns are lessons of physical activity. No education, howsoever ideal and exalted in its objectives, is complete without emphasis on motor activity. The human body is a sacred gift of Nature. Its growth, development and efficiency largely depends upon the quantity and quality of motor activities it performs. Compartmentalization of human personality into "body, mind, and spirit" is an over-simplification.

The mind and spirit do not reveal themselves without body. The body, being an observable material cause of mind, is an instrument through which man performs all mundane duties enjoined upon him by Nature and society.

Physical Education is an integral part of the total educational program of each student. Through the medium of sport and movement all students will participate in a sequential, differentiated program that fosters each student's personal health, fitness and safety. Through exposure to a wide variety of activities, students will gain the necessary knowledge to understand the importance of and make educated decisions around opportunities to achieve and maintain a healthy lifestyle.

Any reputed physical education institute is committed to and supports the development of a positive and appropriate values driven education. Social skills which include but are not limited to respect, cooperation, communication, teamwork and sportsmanship are an important aspect of the Physical Education curriculum and will be directly taught throughout the student's school career.

The values, principles and concepts associated with a quality physical education program surpass the boundaries of the gymnasium and playing fields. Physical activity is a catalyst for learning in all content areas.

Physical education must not be simply supervised playtime. Defining a coherent physical education philosophy, developing a comprehensive program that will meet desired goals, and hiring teachers who "buy into" these ideals are vital to the success of a physical education program. It is only when this has been accomplished that students are provided with an ongoing learning process that enables them to discover their own potential and maximize their chances for self-fulfillment."

In physical education the student should be the most important aspect. Physical education should be a student centered course that allows for students to experience a substantial amount of learning and realize as well as experience the benefits of a physically active and healthy lifestyle. It needs to educate, encourage and help students to improve their physical fitness. It should be an inclusive course were all participants are welcome, encouraged and feel safe. It needs to be adaptive so that all skill levels and learning capacities are accommodated. A place where students are taught about transfer and interdisciplinary learning occurs.

Physical education should promote goal-setting,

teamwork, respect, and responsibility. Students should be provided with motivation to accomplish these goals, work well with their peers, respect themselves, and take on responsibility. They should gain valuable personal and social skills that will benefit them for the rest of their lives. Physical education also needs to educate students on the basic movement patterns to help them build a solid base which allows for safe participation in lifelong physical activity.

It needs to be taught by an active, engaging, and caring physical educator who promotes lifelong learning to all students. The teacher should act as a facilitator and help students in achieving objectives and goals. The teacher needs to deliver the curriculum through effective teaching strategies and effectively evaluate.

Lastly, it is essential that physical education is fun, exciting, and challenging!

8

PHYSICAL EDUCATION AND SPORTS AS A SOCIAL INSTITUTIONS

Sports are a physical activity occurs in a given cultural mailer and is socially structured. Human individual is a social being and he develop and prayers in society. An individual perform any physical activity or sports with in the society only. Any physical activity or sport that exists in society viewing its influences group or society. Therefore, physical education and sports cannot its influences on individuals.

It is the subject of sociology that helps us in understanding socialization. Socialization is a process by which individuals learn about their environment and acquire social characteristics.

On the one hand socialization can also be explained as a process of acquiring social values and living together on the other hand physical education and sports also deals with learning of social values and collective performances.

Therefore, sociology having great importance in the field of physical education and sports. Following are some importance in the filed of physical education and sports.

1. Sports as a Social Phenomena

Sociology focuses on sports as social phenomena. Influences of sports on an individual or society are importantly analyzed through various social aspects. Sociology deals with individuals, groups which also engaged in sports. Sociology helps in understanding every aspect of these social phenomena. It therefore helps in the upliftment and better understanding of sports in the society.

2. Sports Ethics

Sociology develops social valves in individuals or groups, which directly or indirectly enhances sports ethics in an athlete. An athlete is a social being; .He applies the learned social valves in sports and shows good sportsman spirit. In the filed of sports ethics (fair play, respect etc.) is highly required and sociology plays great role in it.

3. Role Play

The process of socialization teaches us "Role play" as an important aspect. Every social being is essentially comes under the aspect. Role-play. Realization and understanding the responsibilities by an individual makes the society healthy and more progressive. Similarly in the filed of physical Education and sports 'Role-playing' learned through socialization is very important.

4. Quality Sports

Social valves, ethics status developed through socializations helps in providing us quality sports. For the development of physical education and sports, sociology assists in providing quality sports to society.

Quality sports are the need of hour this can help in the development of the field of physical Education and sports.

5. Cooperation and Competition

Cooperation and competition are two important characteristics of socialization that exist in society. Sociology give importance to both aspects and in sports both exist together. Sociology teaches us that cooperation's as important as competition in society. Sports also required good and healthy relationship between competition and cooperation. Sociology aware us about their importance in society and in the field of physical education and sports.

6. Sports Become More Educative

Sociology makes sports and games more educative and valuable for the sports persons or society. Sociology teaches us social values and importance of healthy relationships, sports further strengthens the social values. It is not possible for any athlete to develop good cooperation and sportsmanship with out understanding social values. Hence, sociology plays important role in making sports more educative and valuable for the society.

7. Social Control and Self-Discipline

In the field of sports many times spectators go out of control and this may lead to heavy mass causalities. Many times in European football league such uncontrolled situation has existed. The discipline of sociology develops the collective sense of discipline and social control. Crucial matches or tournament require this collective sense of discipline and social control. Therefore for a successful finishing of crucial tournaments factors under sociology like social control and self discipline is highly required.

8. Group Dynamics

More the sociological effect on team members more will be the group dynamics. To work in same team or group and putting all effort collectively to gain good performance as a team/or group require group dynamics .Sociology has given much importance on this aspect of socialization and this shows the importance of sociology in the field of physical education and sports.

9. Individual as Social Beings

Sociology helps individual to become a valuable member of a society. It enables a man to be good social being and a good social being understands the importance of social values and ethics in the field of physical education and sports.

Sociology make athletes understand what kind of behaviour is acceptable to society and what not, this helps him to become a good sports person.

10. Improves Standard of Sports

Through social factors like good character, discipline, self-control, loyalty, Nationalism, respect etc. in the field of physical education and sports standard of sports also increases. The process of socialization assists in developing good sports ethics in society. Unfair attitude, Doping cases, Negative remarks etc., unsocial behaviour reduces through socialization and this no doubt increasing the standard of sports.

11. Achievement and Performance in Sports Increases

Healthy social relations with team members and

others and good cooperative behaviour build confidence and motivation in players. Group Dynamics is considered an important factor for good performance of any team. Team cannot neglect the importance of social values for good performance and achievements. Sociological aspects plays important role in gaining high performance by any team or group.

12. Interdependence of Sociology and Physical Education or Sports

Physical Education and sports more strengthen the social values learned under sociology. Sports give more practical experience to the process of socialization. In physical Education and sports one get enough opportunities to implement and understand social values learned under sociology Physical Education and sports no doubt enhances the process of socialization.

13. Sociology of Sports

Sociology of sports is an area of sociology that informs us about influences of physical Education and sports on society. Therefore sociology also explains the impact of sport participation on the life of a person or society as a whole. Importance of sociology itself exists when we remind the statement "Sports is a social phenomenon".

ROLE OF PHYSICAL EDUCATION AND SPORTS IN SOCIO-CULTURAL HERITAGE

Culture is a belief, a practice, a custom, which has its root in the past and has been transmitted from the past generation to their succeeding generation. Each nation having its own values or practices and as these valves or practices are accepted by the new generation, it becomes their cultural heritage, i.e. YOGA, it was practiced by our ancestors and they perform it as a sacred workout. Slowly it becomes tradition in Indian culture. Now a days Yoga is a popular sport also and we having competitions in Yoga at various levels. This strengthens the belief that Games and sports is our cultural Heritage.

Several games now familiar across the world are their origin as culture of one or the other society (nation). ARCHERY was well-accepted culture of many Nations in Ancient time, which has now existed as very popular and competent sport. In India chess, playing cards, Gully Danda, Kabbadi etc., were very existing as modified sports and games.

Even if we talk about basic human activities like walking, running, jumping, throwing etc., were as essential to human beings in ancient time as these are now a days. All such kind of survival activities become part of our culture dances like Bharatanatyam, Bhangra, Kathak, Katha Kali, Kuchipudi etc., show Indian culture and on the side they are good physical activities as well.

Games and sports are correctly considered as very valuable culture of any nation and it must be treated and enhanced as cultural heritage. Following points clears us more about the statement "Games and Sports as man's cultural Heritage"

1. Being passed on generation to generation

Games and sports are rich cultural heritage of every nation, which is being accepted by next generation. Like other culture Games and sports is also a practice or a tradition which has its root in the past and has been transmitted from the past generation to their succeeding generation. Gradually the ancient physical activities existed in a modified manner, as our other culture is also modified. Games and sports has its valves since time immemorial and human beings had grownup in sports culture and this culture is an important heritage of every country.

2. Culture itself as games/Sports

Many classical Indian dances, which are part of our valuable culture since long back, are also good physical activities. Archery Disc throw, racing wrestling etc., comes under ancient culture but these are popular sports also. Gladiatorial Combats in Rome Olympic in Athens Lingiads in Sweden is an important cultural heritage of respective countries but these comes under games and sports as well. Therefore games and sports is also an important cultural heritage.

3. Importance of culture shown in sports

Sports and Games were integral part of many societies and many sports societies and many sports were as culture in many nations. Because of ancient Olympics is culture in Athens, the people there were good sports persons or sports being. In every age we could analyze the influence of culture on sports. Ancient Greeks then consisted of numerous small states, was of very belligerent attitudes and this behaviour existed in their sports activities and tough physical training. Organization of sports athletic events wrestling, racings, throwing etc., by various nations in national festivals shows sports and games as culture. Culture of sports in ancient Greece was always in priority and Truce was observed inspite of their belligerent attitude during the Olympics. It indicate us the moral importance of this cultural heritage.

4. Exchange of culture by sports

There are many such activities like Archery, Wrestling, Throwing, Chess Racing, Martial Arts, Yoga etc., which indicated culture of many societies and at present these activities are well recognized as popular sports. Many Indian cultural programmes (like Yoga Bhangra, kathak) are beneficial physical activities. It is some times therefore hard to differentiate between culture and sports.

5. Modification of Culture

A game named CHATURANG was an important part of ancient Indian culture, now known as CHESS is the modification of culture. Sports and Games were integral part of every nation's culture and modification is the requirement. But this modification doesn't changes the culture. The sports like chess, archery, wrestling, and racings etc., were an important part of culture in past also and will remain an important part in future also.

Games and Sports as main cultural heritage

It is no doubt that "Games and sports" is cultural heritage of every nation. Since from ancient time human being is well involved in physical activities in one or the other form.

Hunting was activity for survival of primitive man, later existed as famous sport of Javelin, shooting etc., the best way to prove given statement "Games and sports an man's cultural heritage is going to Historical Background of physical activities in different nations.

1. GREECE- Greece has contributed a lot in making games and sports as cultural heritage. Greece was the first nation who adopted sports competitions as National

Festivals. History of Greece (in Games and sports mainly) can be divided in four sports-

i. Homeric period.

ii. Spartan period

iii. Early Athenian period

iv. Later Athenian period.

i. Homeric period. This period has recorded early Grecian life, where a great interest of people is found towards physical activities like wrestling, shooting, chariot Races, gymnastics. Other cultural activities like dancing, arts were also famous needed physical involvements.

ii. Spartan period. Spartans were basically strict followers of military regulations. They are recognized as Man of action. Touch physical activities was the regular programme for every individual. Every effort was made to keep them physically fit. Wrestling, jumping, throwing were their famous sports. Spartan had introduced Ball games also.

iii. Early Athenian Period- Early Athenian were democratic in nature but they never underestimated military abilities. Here also tough physical activities were essential part of educational curriculum. They were famous for celebrating mainly four national athletic contests (Pannellenic games).

a) Olympic- In honour of God Zeus celebrated every first year of Olympiad.

b) Pythian games- in honour of God Apollo. Celebrated every 3rd year of Olympiad.

c) Isthmian games- In honour of God of sea, celebrated

every 2nd and 4th year of Olympiad.

d) Neemean games- In honour of God Zeus celebrated every 2nd years of Olympiad.

iv. Later Athenian period- this period generally known as Golden period. By this period sports existed as profession also. Apart from physical activities, other concerning activities related with fitness and health became; popular like medical Gymnastics, corrective exercises.

Rome- In early Rome physical activities used for improving skills of war, getting courage. Dance was an integral event of their cultural programme. Combat sports like wrestling, sword fighting were very famous earlier but then existed the brutal gladiatorial combats 264 BC. Chariot races, throwing events and minor children recreational games were also on demand. Gambling was also very famous in Roman society. Thermac (thermal Bath-rooms) was in good utilization for recreation or relaxation.

Germany- Germany has contribute a lot in making games and sports as world's cultural heritage by giving new concepts in physical activities.

Johan -B. Basedow (1713-1790) who is recognized as founder of modern physical Education pvt. Every effort to popularize physical activities in schools.

Johann Guts Muths (1959-1839) who is regarded as father of German gymnastics introduced gymnastics in schools and popularized other like swimming, wrestling, balance exercises, hiking as part of physical Educational programme. Guts Muths also introduces Recreational activities for better development of personality.

Activities like Football, gymnastics, swimming, indoor games are extremely popular in Germany.

Japan

Physical activities mainly defensive art exists clearly within the culture of Japan. Fencing, Japanese wrestling, archery, obscuring hunting are very cultural and exists since ancient time. Budo (Military art) was very religious also since 1880 when Professor Jigard Kend who invented Judo many traditional schools are teaching this defensive activity has become part of their culture.

Sweden

Gymnastics, Fencing, Swimming are regarded as their traditional activities. Medical gymnastics (exercises for good body posture) is also famous. Weather conditions do not favour outdoor games much but winter sports like skating are popular since long back. Indoor games are therefore more close to people here. In Sweden 'Lingiad' named after 'per Henrik Ling' is celebrated as sports festival.

Denmark

Denmark is the first European country to make games and sports or physical activities as essential programme in school curriculum. Rifle club was formed to teach shooting and military drills in Denmark . Traditional Danis gymnastic (Rhythmic exercises) has become world famous.

USA

Sports and games is in culture of U.S.A. since ancient time. With little modification and need of people many games like Basket ball (1892), Volley Ball (1892),

American Foot ball, Baseball, Handball, Rugby, Golf introduced in U.S.A. Track field and gymnastic is also very popular. Combat sports (Wrestling, boxing etc.) is in demand always. Physical education is compulsory subject in schools in America.

India

Games and sports in ancient India since Vedic age (2000-1000 B.C.) is regarded as very prestigious and royal activity. Archery, horse riding, chariot racing, gambling were very popular activities slowly passed on to whole world. Yoga (Yug) is traditional activity in India performed by every one. In Epic age Gurukuls Physical activity was performed regularly. Indian warriors were specialized in Archery, wrestling, sword fighting, disc throwing Javelin throwing etc. Kho Kho, Kabaddi etc., are very famous and regarded as indigenous games. Folk dance of every state involves lot of physical workout. India has also introduced many Rhythmic exercises and mass display like BHARTIUM. World famous game of Badminton is discovered in India. Cricket, Soccer, Volley ball, Basket ball are other famous games.

Sociological approach and Value Education through Physical Education Programme

If the aim of Education is enrichment of personality, Physical Education contributes to much extent. If the aim of Education is self/ realization, again no doubt physical Education provides opportunities to develop the sense of self/ realization. To achieve every philosophical realization aim and objective of Education, physical, Education play an important role and assist in developing those objectives more practically. Therefore, it is said that physical education is an integral part of total education process.

Whole Educational process become more easy and efficient when physical Education put its contributions physical education is an essential part of total education process. Secondary Education Commission (1952-53) enlisted four aims of education i.e.

(i) Development of democratic approach,

(ii) Improvement of vocational efficiency,

(iii) Development of personality and

(iv) Development of qualities of leadership.

Physical education puts its great contribution in developing these qualities in an individual.

Two statements 'A sound mind lies in a sound body' and 'physical Education an integral part of total Education' is one statement empowers the other statement. A complete personality is consisted of healthy body and healthy mind. In other words it can be said physical educations assist whole educational process in developing all round personality. Only theoretical approach may produce a sound mind, but for a sound body physical approach is required. Therefore only class room education itself cannot be considered as a complete educational programme until and unless physical education is regarded as an integral part of the programme. Relationship of physical education with general education is well recognized and understood. It is therefore, physical education found essentially place in regular curriculum of every education institution.

Following given points present, the assistance of physical education in valuing education.

1. Interesting- sports and games, recreation and other physical activities create interest in students and they become motivated to follow educational programmes. Physical Education makes education programme more interesting. Physical education is a source recreation, relaxation; keep students happy and enjoyable, which make students energetic and interesting in the total educational programmes.

2. Effective and easy learning

Only classroom learning in an educational programme may not be much effective. Learning of social valves like cooperation, adjustment, teamwork, self-control etc. is more effective and practical in physical education. Student's participation in different physical activities provides ample opportunities to learn many educational valves. Therefore physical education assist total education programme in effective and easy learning of students.

3. Healthy approach

Physical education develops competitive spirit with a cooperative attitude. This aspect bring programme in the total education programme. Students try to perform their best in classrooms or in Examinations with a cooperative attitude. Apart from this, physical activities make students physical fit and mentally healthy. This can be concluded as physical education makes total education programme a healthy approach.

4. Responsibilities and Discipline

Physical Education through its various activities assists in developing sense of responsibility and discipline in students. These qualities make possible the smooth and effective running of education programmes. Therefore, total education programme possibly achieve the motive of producing valuable citizens for the country.

5. Knowledge

Physical education coves wide range of subjects like Physiology, human anatomy, psychology, sport medicine, health education etc., which involve huge knowledge for the students. Learning of healthy education first aid, communicable diseases, diet and nutrition like topics is very essential for children's and adolescents. Updating of knowledge is one of the main objectives of any education programme. Physical Education contributes a lot also in relation to providing beneficial knowledge to students.

6. Growth and Development

During the phases of infant to adolescent individual requires special attention for their proper growth and development. Absence of any physical activities may harm the normal growth and development. In this stage students require some specific kind of physical activities, which assist in their growth and development. Education curriculum must be involve such activities for proper growth and development of students.

7. Friendship and Relationship

Sports and other physical activities provide an environment for every one to feel enjoyable and understand each other. Physical education assist in strength ring relationships and develop the quality of group dynamics it improves student - student and student - teacher relationship Good relations bring progress in the total education programme.

8. Other

Physical education develops many other such qualities behaviour or attitude that make physical education an important part of total education programme. Physical education develops leadership qualities, and personal habits acceptable attitude. Creativeness in students.

Physical education therefore plays an important role in putting the value education.

SOCIAL STRATIFICATION AND SPORTS

In sociology and other social sciences, social stratification refers to the hierarchical arrangement of individuals into divisions of power and wealth within a society. Stratification derives from the geological concept of strata - rock layers created by natural processes. The term most commonly relates to the socio-economic concept of class, involving the "classification of persons into groups based on shared socio-economic conditions ... a relational set of inequalities with economic, social, political and ideological dimensions."

In modern Western societies, stratification is typically described as a composition of three main layers: upper class, middle class, and lower class. Each class may be further subdivided into smaller classes (e.g. occupational). These categories are particular to state-level societies as distinguished from, for instance, feudal societies composed of nobility-to-peasant relations. Stratification may also be defined by kinship ties or castes. For Max Weber, social class pertaining broadly to material wealth is distinguished from status class based on honour, prestige, religious affiliation, and so on. It is debatable whether the earliest hunter-gatherer groups may be defined as 'stratified', or if such differentials began with agriculture and broad acts of exchange between groups. To this extent society may begin with stratification itself, and vice versa. One of the ongoing issues in determining social stratification arises from the point that status inequalities between individuals are common, so it becomes a quantitative issue to determine how much inequality qualifies as stratification.

Sociological Overview

The concept of social stratification is interpreted differently by the various theoretical perspectives of sociology. Proponents of structural-functionalism have suggested that since social stratification is commonly found in developed societies, hierarchy may be necessary in order to stabilize social structure. Talcott Parsons, an American sociologist, asserted that stability and social order are achieved by means of a universal value consensus, satisfying the functional prerequisites of a society. By contrast, conflict theories, such as Marxism, point to the inaccessibility of resources and lack of social mobility found in stratified societies. Many sociological theorists have criticized the extent to which the working classes are unlikely to advance socioeconomically; the wealthy tend to hold political power which they use to exploit the proletariat intergenerationally. Theorists such as Ralf Dahrendorf, however, have noted the tendency toward an enlarged middle-class in modern Western societies due to the necessity of an educated workforce in technological and service economies. Various social and political perspectives concerning globalization, such as dependency theory, suggest that these effects are due to the shift of workers to the third world.

The impact of class stratification on sports participation. Each society established has its own set of norms, values, and beliefs. It is these that have instigated societies to transform and develop over time creating principles of inequality, prejudice and segregation. This development is evident within the sporting world, as society repeatedly forces discrimination and segregation based on socio-economic or physical differences. Sport has been utilized and persistent in a modern society characterised by profound forms of social stratification. Social or class stratification, is possibly the utmost initiator of disparity. Reid (1977) considered social stratification as an “arrangement of society into layers”. However, this usually implies some form of segregation or comparative evaluation of the layer. Indications can be made not only to differentiate groups within a society, but to a hierarchy or ranking of these groups. Therefore social stratification produces classes commonly identified as, the upper-class, middle-class and working-class.

So throughout the generation it is like the main area of sport I think that's why I love the game so much, as it's been drilled into me. Each objective characteristic can be stereotypically associated with one's position in society. It is apparent that social factors such as gender, age, race culture etc, are not well considered, and in fact neglected when discussing class and society. A strong belief of sociologists such as Houlihan. Consensus within a social order is believed to have effect in a Functionalist's society. For the working class, trying to improve one's importance in society is highly unachievable. 2002, The Sociology of Sport and Physical

Education. 1999, Understanding Sport: An introduction to the sociological and cultural analysis of sport, E & FN SPON, London. This could be suggested as suspicious or extremely careless, when he holds such a high status is sport, and sets an example to others. Yeah my dad, my granddad, his dad, so my great grand dad he played for Arsenal. I'm really proud of my achievements. However, in contrast, the Proletariat is completely estranged.

9

IMPORTANCE OF SPORTS PSYCHOLOGY IN PHYSICAL EDUCATION

Meaning of Psychology

Field of psychology is considered to be originated from Aristotle's treatise named De anima. For the first time, word psychology was used by Rudolf Goeckel, who used it for study of mind of a living organism. Thus, the concept of psychology got originate in the year 1590.

If we look at literal meaning of psychology, then it will be found that this word came into being from combination of two words, namely, psyche and logos, which are Greek words. In simple language, psyche implies soul of a being while logos stands for act of talking or studying. Thus meaning of word originated from combination of these words will be study of sole of a being. After it's coming into being, this concept became widely used and since then, it has not lost its originality.

In ancient Greek, greater importance was provided to study of sole, as they considered sole as essence of the organism. After that, various experts spent their time for understanding true nature of psychology and it was because of such studies that people began to differentiate between mental and spiritual aspects of soul. Various experts considered observable aspect of soul more importance in comparison to spiritual aspect. Observal aspect of soul was termed as mind. On this basis, some of experts defined the psychology as study of the human minds. However, on this issue, a split is being found among experts. Experts of other school considered psychology to be study of consciousness as according to them, consciousness is nothing but private domain of a human being into which no one can peak with naked eyes. However, as consciousness does not have any objective form, because of which it is not possible to study it with objective means. If someone is asked to note down the feelings which arise in him when he is sad, it is possible that he or she cannot perform this task properly as feelings and emotions are not stable and they keep on changing from time to time. This is the main reason that various experts are of the view that feelings, which are unstable, cannot be studied because of which they cannot be considered as field of psychology in any way.

There are some experts who consider that mind of living organisms is composed of two distinctive parts, namely, conscious as well as unconscious. There are various acts which a human being perform in conscious state while various acts are performed by him or her in an unconscious state. In psychology, both the states of mind, namely, conscious and unconscious, should be studied, as without these it is not possible to understand behaviour of an individual properly. One such theory was provided by Sigmund Freud.

Another important theory of psychology was provided by an expert named Watson. According to his theory, psychology was an objective science which helps to study the behaviour of living organisms, which is objective and subjective. His theory was based on the assumption that whatever an individual does, his or her inner being is get reflected in those activities.

To explain concept of psychology, an expert commented that psychology is that science which is used to study the activities performed by an individual in relation to his or her environment. According to this expert, various environmental forces affect inner and outer activities of human beings in various ways because of which it becomes important for the psychologist to study conscious as well as unconscious activities performed by an individual.

Various experts view psychology from different perspectives, by which boundaries have been demarcated in which concept of psychology can be used, which are as follows :—

a. As Science : Various experts consider psychology to be a science. This view is based on the notion that science is trained and organised form of common sense. In science, systematic approach is used for solving out various kinds of problems. In this field, cause and effect relationship is developed to understand the reason of various facts.

Today, various branches of knowledge have been developed and on basis of their nature and scope, they have been classified into specific groups. Like various other fields, psychology is considered to be a positive science. In psychology, things are analysed in the manner in which they exist. Now, psychology has attained a objective form and it is no longer only a subjective field. In psychology, certain norms have been laid down which explains that in different kinds of situations how a person will react. Psychology is only concerned with that how a human being reacts in a particular situation and not with the fact that how he should react. It is only concerned with explaining the cause of the way in which a person reacts. As like science, psychology tries to develop a relationship between cause and effect, it is considered as a positive science by some of the experts.

b. As Environment : All the objects and conditions in which a human being lives and grows is known as environment. Various environmental factors affect growth and development of human beings to a lot of extent. These factors play an important role in determining physical structure pattern of human beings and it also defines the kind of functions they perform.

In the light of prevailing environment, it is possible to compare the life-style of modern man and that of primitive man. Today, it is even possible to analyse the manner in which they used to behave in certain specific situations. Innate behaviour of a person can be modified to a lot of extent by the kind of environment in which he lives. Without considering the kind of environment in which a person lives, his behaviour cannot be studied properly.

c. As Individual : All the living individuals possess various physical and mental qualities and they are product of combination of these qualities. Some of the experts are of view that psychology is concerned with study of mind of a person, however, this is inadequate aspect of the subject as human body and soul are related directly to each other. When we talk about any individual, we take into account his mental and physical attributes. A person's behaviour is determined by his mind and body interactions. All individuals are made up of heredity and environment, because of which both of them affect a person's personality to a lot of extent.

As said earlier that concept of psychology applies only on human beings as animals cannot organise a society and without concept of society, there cannot be any concept of personality. Human beings have to spent their life in an environment which keeps on changing from time to time. To live a comfortable life, they are required to make adjustments in themselves so that they can adapt themselves according to changed conditions. On the basis of behaviour pattern of an individual, experts try to understand personality of the person. As various kinds of individual differences are found among human beings because of which no results can obtained if they are being studied commonly. It is necessary to study all the individuals as individual only then proper results can be obtained.

Sports psychology is that branch of psychology that deals with the behaviour of athlete on and off the ground. Sports psychology is the study of behaviour of sports persons in training and competition periods. It is a subject which provides us the information about he influence of sports on sports persons behaviour and the influence of sports persons behaviour on sports performance. This subject deals with the behaviour of sports persons in various situations with an aim of enhancing his/her sports performance.

Sports psychology now days existing as very valuable discipline which playing important role in understanding sports person and improving sports performance. Sports psychology deals with the behaviour of related individuals on the play ground sports psychology tries to enhance the performance of sports persons by developing required sense of various psychological aspects, like stress management during competitions, over coming nervousness at de^buts etc.

To train or prepare an athlete for competition is not an individual matter. As Bio/Mechanists to work on mechanical skills and related works, Nutritionists to work on diet management, coach to work on technique, tactics, strategies and other related works, Psychologists are equally important and required for maintaining and developing psychological aspects to lead a good athlete. It is a science that provides motivation and counselling to the players, coaches, officials in other improve the field of games and sports.

Various psychological factors like Motivation, Aggression, and attitude, Anxiety, Interest etc. no doubt put their influence on athlete and his performance. The science of sports psychology deals with the athlete in these aspects. Sports psychology improves the performance of athletes by approaching positively through these various aspects of psychology. This branch of psychology assesses the behaviour of persons related directly or indirectly with sports and work for the development of this field. Sports psychology having its three main sub branches i.e. -

a) Educational sports psychology- This division concentrates on educating various sports psychological aspects to Athletes, coaches, officials, organizer's and other related bodies of sports and games. This involves the interest, demands and requirements, influences of athletes, fans and spectators on the field of sports. Hence

Educational sports psychology is said to be making "sports settings."

b) Research sports Psychology- This division concentrate on Experimental works on sports psychology field. This involves the various psychological aspects to research on and verify its influences on sports or athletes. Research sports psychology undertakes athlete's behavioural aspects and its influences on sports or athletes. Research sports psychology undertakes on sports performance. In this division research work is processed to enhance the field of sports and games.

c) Clinical sports psychology-This division concentrates on remedial aspects in the field of sports. This deals with the approaches to overcome the athlete's problems and assist them to increase the performance. Clinical sports psychology efforts to improve athlete's sports performance by providing them appropriate and effective counselling.

Coleman Griffith is the father of sports psychology. He contributed a lot in the upliftment of sports through this discipline and put an importance to sports psychology, which is well applauded and recognized by the world.

Definitions

1. "Sports psychology is a science in which principles of psychology are applied in sport setting, to enhance performance."

—Richard H.Cox

2. "Sports Psychology is the application of psychological principles to sport and physical activity at all levels of skill improvement."
—M. Brown

3. "Sports Psychology is related to the ability to understand athlete performance and to improve exercise programmes."
—N. Singer

4. "Sports psychology is a division of general psychology apply psychological facts and principles to learning performance and associated human behaviour in the field of sports".
—John Lavther

5. "Sports psychology is the sports science that govern the quality of performance and shows that psychological factors and procedures to produce performance enhancement effects."
—S. Rusha

Different Branches of Psychology

Today, field of psychology has grown to a lot of extent and these days, it is being used as a means to understand and to modify human behaviours according to the prevailing environment. All the fields of human behaviour are being studied in psychology. Earlier it entered only in the fields of education and industry, however, now it has made its place in the fields of physical education and sports.

This use of psychology in various diverse areas has led to development of concept of applied psychology through which this can be used for practical purposes. Today's life is full of problems and pressures and in this kind of situation, it has become very important to study the behavioural problems of human beings. The main reason of arising such kind of problems is that human beings find it very difficult to make adjustments with the changed environment. In this kind of situation, it has become very important to provide the knowledge as to how one can adjust himself or herself in complex situations. As said earlier, today psychology has entered the area of physical education and sports as well, and plays a very important role in understanding psychology of sportsmen.

Meaning and Nature of Sports Psychology

Hardly a subject associated with sport is more intriguing than the subject of sport psychology. Perhaps this is because it is a comfortable subject for so many people associated with sport. The average spectator does not care to offer a biomechanical explanation for why an athlete achieves a linear superhuman feat, yet the same spectator is often more than willing to give a psychological explanation. In many ways tis is good, but it is also the reason any athletes and coaches don't feel the need for a professional sport psychologist on their team.

Generally question is asked by some people that whether sports psychologist can learn something about performance enhancement from coach of team. In reality, successful coaches and athletes are people who make it a point to study their sport and master the mental elements of the game. This process can be speeded up and refined through the correct application of the scientific principles of sport psychology. It is found that elite athletes generally recognize the need for a professional sport psychologist. This perception was observed to increase as athletes came into actual contact with sport psychologists' services.

Sport Psychology Defined

Sport psychology is a science in which the principles of psychology are applied in a sport or exercise setting. These principles are often applied to enhance performance. However, the true sport psychologist is interested in much more than performance enhancement and sees sport as a vehicle for human enrichment. A wit-at-all-costs attitude is inconsistent with the goals and aspirations of the best sport psychologist. It is possible that a quality sport experience can enhance an athlete's intrinsic motivation without the athlete necessarily winning. Taken as a whole, sport psychology is an exciting subject dedicated to the enhancement of both athletic performance and the social-psychological aspects of human enrichment.

Development of Sports Psychology

Sport psychology as a field of study is extremely young and still evolving. The first clear example of historical research being conducted in the area of sport psychology was reported by Norman Triplett. Drawing upon field observations and secondary data, Triplett analyzed the performance of lists under conditions of social facilitation. He concluded from this milestone research that the presence of other competitors was capable of facilitating better cycling performance. While Triplett provided an example of one of the earliest recorded sport psychology investigations, he was not the first person to systematically carry out sport psychology research over an extended period of time. This distinction is generally attributed to Coleman Roberts Griffith, often referred to as the father of sport psychology in America. Griffith is credited with establishing the first sport psychology laboratory at the University of Illinois in 1925. Over an extended period of time, Griffith studied the nature of psychomotor skills, motor learning, and the relationship between personality variables and motor performance.

It was not until the 1960s that sport psychology began to emerge as separate and distinct from other areas of motor behaviour research. It was only after the Second World War the American universities began to offer courses in the parent discipline of motor learning. Such notables as Franklin M. Henry at the University of California, John Lawther at Pennsylvanial State University, and Arthur Slater-Hammel at Indiana University pioneered these courses.

Another significant event in the 1960s was the publication of "Problem of Athletes and How to Handle Them" by Bruce Ogilvie and Thomas Tutko. This book and the author's personality inventory for athletes— the Athletic Motivation Inventory— caught on with coaches and athletes. However, Ogilvie and Tutko's work was not well received by the sport psychology is much better received today than it was only a few short years ago. Bruce Ogilvie is referred to as the father of applied sport psychology.

A number of professional sport psychology organizations have evolved since the 1960s. In 1965 the International Society of Sport psychology, which sponsors worldwide meetings and publishers the International Journal of Sport psychology and The Sport Psychology, was organized in Rome. The Purpose of the ISSP is to promote and disseminate information about the practice of sport psychology throughout the world.

In 1965, a small group of physical educators from

Canada and the United States met in Dales, Texas, to discuss the feasibility of forming a professional organization distinct from the American Association of Health, Physical Education, and Recreation. The efforts of this small group came to fruition in 1966 when it was recognized by the ISSP. The name of the new organization became the North American Society for the psychology of sport and Physical Activity. The first annual meeting of NASPSPA was held prior to the 1967 AAHPERD national convention in Las Vegas. Since that time, NASPSPA has evolved into an influential academic society focusing on sport psychology.

NASPSPA's primary goal has been to advance the knowledge base of sport psychology through experimental research. Shortly after the emergence of NASPSPA in the United States, another significant professional organization came into existence in Canada in 1969. This organization was called the Canadian Society for Psychomotor Learning and Sport psychology. CSPLSP was originally organized under the auspices of the Canadian Association for Health, Physical Education, and Recreation, but became an independent society in 1977.

Somewhat concurrently with the emergence of the Canadian association the Sport Psychology Academy emerged in the United States as one of six academies within the National Association for Sport and Physical Education. NASPSE is an association within the AAHPERD. The six academies were formed to represent the knowledge base or disciplines within physical education.

Some times back, two sport psychologies have emerged. The first is referred to as Academic Sport

Psychology and the second as Applied Sport Psychology. The former or traditional sport psychology continues to focus on the disciplinary or research- oriented aspects of the field. Conversely, Applied Sport Psychology focuses on the professional or applied aspects of the field of sport psychology.

The division took place because many sport psychologists who were interested in application did not think NASPSPA was meeting their needs Consequently, the Association for the Advancement of Applied Sport psychology was formed in the fall of 1985.

Medicine and Science in Sports and Exercise is the official journal of the American College of Sports Medicine and regularly publishers articles relating to both exercise and sport. While not associated with any association or society, the Journal of Sport Behaviour and the Journal of Interdisciplinary Research in Physical Education publish exercise and sport psychology research.

A split took place in the American Psychological Association, resulting in the formation of the American Psychological Society. In this case, however, dissatisfied academic research psychologists complained that the APA had become too application-oriented. They worried that clinical and applied psychology was being emphasized at the expense of science and research. In 1986, the APA formed yet another section within its structure called Division 47, which is dedicated to issues dealing with exercise and sport psychology. In years to come, the future of applied sport psychology will be greatly influenced by the success of and directions taken by this new organization.

Historically, sport psychology emerged as a discipline from physical education. In recent years, however, a significant interest in the discipline has developed among individuals prepared in psychology and counseling. This has raised the issue among practicing sport psychology as to which people are qualified to call themselves "sport psychologists" and to provide services to athletes.

Some have gone so far as to argue that only licensed psychologists should be allowed to call themselves sport psychologists, and suggest that the appropriate title for a non-licensed sport psychologist would be mental training consultant. Most agree, however, than even licensed psychologists should have significant academic training in the exercise and sport sciences before practicing applied sport psychology.

A partial solution to the issue of professionalization of sport psychology was presented by the United States Olympic Committee and clarified by May. The USOC developed the Sport psychology Registry to identify three categories in which a person can demonstrate competence. These categories correspond to three types of sport psychologists: the Clinical/counseling sport psychologist, the educational sport psychologist, and the research sport psychologist. The purpose of the Sports Psychology Registry was to identify individuals in the area of sport psychology who could work with specific national team within the Olympic movement. The registry was not meant to be a licensing or authorizing committee.

The AAASP took the issue of who is qualified to deliver sport psychology services one step further. It adopted a certification document outlining the process an individual must take to be given the title Certified Consultant, Association for the Advancement of Applied Sport psychology. As part of the certification criteria, the applicant is required to hold an earned doctorate in an area related to sport psychology. In addition, numerous specific courses and experiences are identified. While this certification process adopted by the AAASP may not be the final one, it is good beginning since it recognizes that an individual needs specialized training in psychology and physical education to be certified as a practicing sport psychologist.

It should be mentioned, however, that not all sport psychologists are in agreement about the merits of the AAASP certification process. Anshel, for example, argued that the AAASP certification process is discriminatory and counterproductive. He argues that there is scant evidence that certified consultants make better consultants than non-certified consultants. Nevertheless, it appears that the AAASP certification initiative is a move in the right direction. It requires both licensed and unlicensed psychologists to meet minimum standards in order to be certified by the AAASP.

Importance of Sports Psychology in Physical Education

In an effort to promote the virtues of sport psychology to coaches, athletes, and prospective students, many thoughtful professionals have suggested contributions than sport psychologists can make to sport and physical education. Different roles and functions of the sport psychologist are outlined here. Generally, these roles and functions describe the sport psychologist in the categories of educator and researcher.

(a) The Clinical/Counseling Sport Psychologists

The clinical/Counseling sport psychologist is a person trained in clinical or counseling psychology and is a licensed psychologist. Generally, the clinical sport psychologist also has a deep interest in and understanding of the athletic experience. Training may also include course-work and experience in sport psychology form programs in physical education. Clinical sport psychologists are individuals who are prepared to deal with emotional and personality disorder problems that affect some athletes. The athletic experience can be very stressful to some athletes, and can negatively affect their performance of their ability to function as healthy human beings. In these cases, sport psychologists trained in counselling psychology or clinical psychology are needed.

(b) The Educational Sport Psychologists

Most sport psychologists who received their academic training through departments of physical education consider themselves to be educational sport psychologists. These individuals have mastered the knowledge base of sport psychology and serve as practitioners. They use the medium of education to teach correct principles of sport psychology to athletes and coaches. In general, their mission and role is to help athletes develop psychological skills for performance enhancement. The also help athletes, young and old, to enjoy sport and use it as a vehicle for improving their quality of life.

(c) The Research Sport Psychologist

For sport psychology to be a recognized and respected social science, the knowledge base must continue to grow. It is the scientist and scholar who serves this important role. For the practicing sport psychologist to enjoy professional credibility, there must exist a credible scientific body of knowledge.

Human beings are considered to be extremely complex structures and functions performed by them are also unimaginable. Various studies have been conducted by experts to find out the factors which affect or control stress lingering upon human beings. In sports also, sports psychologist tries to control these factors as no player under stress can perform well.

Since a long time, various experts were of the view that behaviours of players should be studied. If coach evaluates the personal qualities or players before beginning coaching, then he can get good results. Areas of physical education and psychology are related to each other as through education, a teacher tries to modify student's behaviour, while a psychologist tries to study behaviour of human being in relating to his or her environment. Unless teacher does not have knowledge of behaviour of players, he cannot modify it in any way.

In sports activities, all the players are required to learn various kinds of complex motor skills. For proper performance, he or she has to modify the behaviour in accordance with environment. An individual can realise aim of his or her life only by modifying basic behavioural patterns. To understand behaviour of players, field of psychology is being used by the coaches. Through this tool, a coach tries to make positive modifications in behavioural patterns of the players.

It is very necessary for a coach to have basic knowledge of child's psychology. Through this, he realises the fact that various kinds of developments take place in children, however, in adult's such kind of development processes do not take place, because of which they have attained a stabilized position. Because of this reason, it is easy to modify a child's behaviour, however, a greater difficulty is faced to modify an adult's behaviour. Thus, various kinds of differences exist between children and adults, and coaching should be provided while keeping those differences in mind. Thus with the help of psychology, coaches learn the art of drawing a line between adults and children and also helps them to chose different coaching methods for individual players.

By making use of psychology, sports coaches can draw a programme of physical activities efficiently and can get the best possible results. Through this, coaches can understand strengths and weakness of players and can make use of that coaching technique with which they can grow to maximum extent. Sports psychology helps the coaches as well as the players to introspect each other. Without introspection, no coach can modify player's behaviours. Thus, it can be said that without the study of psychology, it is impossible to plan educational experiences. Only with the knowledge of psychology, a coach can formulate realistic programmes and policies. To create outstanding players, it is necessary that coach himself should have knowledge of his inner being. Only through such kind of knowledge he can understand player's feelings, his strengths and weaknesses. Thus it can be said that with knowledge of psychology, only a strong and meaningful relationship can be established between players and coach.

Various kinds of differences exist in human beings because of which their ability to perform same task differs. Even in sporting abilities, no two players are found to be alike. The main reason of such difference is acute individual differences found in human beings. Different traits are found in different human beings which make them different from each other. Human beings react in same situation in different manner because of difference being found in their traits. Thus, it can be said that without knowledge of psychology, no coach can provide training to the players properly. Such kind of coach cannot bring the players out of stress which is being created by diverse and complex situations. Only through sports psychology, a coach can prepare the players to face strèssful conditions easily and to perform outstandingly even in such conditions.

Sport Psychology playing very influensive role in the society and in the field of sports. An athlete's performance in sports, to much extent depends upon its psychological preparation. Performance in sports not only depends on its physical training or capability but psychological aspects also play important role in performance. An athlete if psychologically strong and prepared for the competition, he/she performs good in the competition. In the elite sports competition psychological factors becomes very important. In sports every player tries its best to perform physically well. Physically all the players are strong enough to compete with each other, all then matter is their psychology.

In the general life style, sport psychology put its influence effectively. Sports psychology is not only limited to grounds or competitions only. It assists individuals in tackling and overcoming many problems off the filed also. Sports psychology not only assists in increasing the performance of an athlete but also develops the personality and attitude of the athlete. Following are described some of the important roles of sports psychology.

1. Increases Determination

Sports psychology increases mental aspects like intelligence, reasoning etc., of an individual. Performance of an athlete to much extent depends up his mental approach. If an athlete is mentally not prepared to complete, he/she cannot perform well. Sports psychology through its various psychological strategies increases mental capability of individual /athletes.

2. Confidence Upliftment

Sports psychology prepares individuals for possible responses to any situation that exist. It helps in building confidence and making possible responses. Sports psychology possibly assist in uplifting player's confidence during competitions.

3. Interest of an athlete

An athlete can learn of perform good skills until he/ she is not interested in learning or performing sports psychology analysis an individuals interest, so that the same individual can proceed further to learn game of its interest. Sport psychology assist in maintaining the desired interest in order to learn and perform well.

4. Motivate Individuals

Sports psychology plays important role in positively motivating individuals. Psychology is the positive science of conduct of behaviour. High level of motivation is essentially required to perform well in the competitions. Sports psychology performs well in the competitions. Sports psychology provides positive preceding that motivates athletes to learn and perform well in competitions.

5. Emotional balance

Sports psychology analysis an athlete's emotional states and feelings that indicate the degree to which he/ she is ready to perform in the competitions. Sports psychology helps in bring balanced emotional state of an athlete. It provides opportunities and studies to make plays emotionally fit and ready for competitions.

6. Helps in learning

Sport psychology is a behavioural assessment of an athlete. It provides comfortable situations and environment so that one can learn effectively sport psychology makes learning process easy and interesting.

7. Healthy competitive spirit

Sport psychology helps in maintaining sports ethics and sportsmanship during practice and competitions. It put valve of sports in society by keeping healthy competitive spirit in players.

8. Healthy Relations

Sport psychology manages our relations in society. It is a science of human behaviour and its relationships. Sport psychology play important role in providing healthy environment in the society, which healthy relations occur among plays, with opponents and in society.

9. Appropriate Attitude-

Sport psychology deals with attitude study of

athletes. It predict athlete's behaviour through it attitude. Sport psychology helps in improving thoughts and feelings of a player. It develops appropriate attitude in the player to create interest in practice.

10. It maintain aggression level of players

In sports aggression is needed for better performance, but it must be in a required level. A player through the sports psychology learns to maintain his aggression level. It is true that aggression increases the performance but more uncontrolled aggressions may result in breaching of rules. Under sport psychology athlete learns to maintain aggression during controversial situations.

11. It develop leadership qualities

Sport psychology focuses on variables related athletes and athletic behaviour. It apply the psychological facts and principles to develop leadership qualities and desired human behaviour. Sports psychology provides every op-opportunity to athlete to exist as a leader in the field of sports and in society.

12. It increases performance

Sport psychology is a sport science that govern the quality of performance and implement those psychological factors and procedures that enhances the performance of a player- sport psychology develop these mental or emotional qualities in an athlete that assist him to learn good skills and performer well in sport competitions.

13. Relation between psychology and physiology

Many psychological aspects like anxiety, Arousal, over/excitement, aggression etc., affects our physiological body systems like Blood pressure, heart rate, nervous mechanism etc. In the field of sports we can not prefer physical ability only an essential factor, psychology aspects like attitude, motivation, aggression etc., plays very important role in controlling physiological systems. Sport psychology plays very influensive role in systemic functioning of body physiology.

14. Increases concentration and attention

Sport psychology is an approach, which increases athlete's concentration and attention in order to learn sport skills and perform his best in the competitions. Sport psychology enables athletes to concentrate on skills and tackle the situations with best efforts during game situations. Through proper concentration on sports athlete display skills well and perform better.

Psychology and Physical Education

The increased stress of competitions can cause athletes to react both physically and mentally in a manner that can negatively affect their performance abilities. They may become tense, their heart rates race, they break into a cold sweat, they worry about the outcome of the competition, they find it hard to concentrate on the task in hand.

This has led coaches to take an increasing interest in the field of sport psychology and in particular in the area of competitive anxiety. That interest has focused on techniques that athletes can use in the competitive situation to maintain control and optimise their performance. Once learned, these techniques allow the athlete to relax and to focus his/her attention in a positive manner on the task of preparing for and participating in competition. Psychology is another weapon in the athlete's armoury in gaining the winning edge.

The 4C's

Concentration, confidence, control and commitment (the 4C's) are generally considered the main mental qualities that are important for successful performance in most sports.

- Concentration - ability to maintain focus
- Confidence - believe in one's abilities
- Control - ability to maintain emotional control regardless of distraction
- Commitment - ability to continue working to agreed goals

The techniques of relaxation, centering and mental imagery can assist an athlete to achieve the 4C's.

Concentration

This is the mental quality to focus on the task in hand. If the athlete lacks concentration then their athletic abilities will not be effectively or efficiently applied to the task. Research has identified the following types of attention focus:

- Broad Narrow continuum - the athlete focuses on a large or small number of stimuli
- Internal External continuum - the athlete focuses on internal stimuli (feelings) or external stimuli (ball)

The demand for concentration varies with the sport:

- Sustained concentration - distance running,

cycling, tennis, squash

• Short bursts of concentration - cricket, golf, shooting, athletic field events

• Intense concentration - sprinting events, bobsleigh, skiing

Common distractions are: anxiety, mistakes, fatigue, weather, public announcements, coach, manager, opponent, negative thoughts etc.

Strategies to improve concentration are very personal. One way to maintain focus is to set process goals for each session or competition. The athlete will have an overall goal for which the athlete will identify a number of process goals that help focus on specific aspects of the task. For each of these goals the athlete can use a trigger word (a word which instantly refocuses the athlete's concentration to the goal) e.g. sprinting technique requires the athlete to focus on being tall, relaxed, smooth and to drive with the elbows - trigger word could be "technique"

Athletes will develop a routine for competition that may include the night before, the morning, pre competition, competition and post competition routines. If these routines are appropriately structured then they can prove a useful aid to concentration.

Confidence

Confidence results from the comparison an athlete makes between the goal and their ability. The athlete will have self-confidence if they believe they can achieve their goal. (Comes back to a quote of mine - "You only achieve what you believe").

When an athlete has self confidence they will tend

to: persevere even when things are not going to plan, show enthusiasm, be positive in their approach and take their share of the responsibility in success and fail.

To improve their self confidence, an athlete can use mental imagery to:

• visualise previous good performance to remind them of the look and feel

• imagine various scenarios and how they will cope with them

Good goal setting (challenging yet realistic) can bring feelings of success. If athletes can see that they are achieving their short term goals and moving towards their long term goals then confidence grows.

Confidence is a positive state of mind and a belief that you can meet the challenge ahead - a feeling of being in control. It is not the situation that directly affects confidence; thoughts, assumptions and expectations can build or destroy confidence.

High Self-Confidence

• Thoughts - positive thoughts of success

• Feelings - excited, anticipation, calm, elation, prepared

• Focus - on self, on the task

• Behaviour - give maximum effort and commitment, willing to take chances, positive reaction to set backs, open to learning, take responsibility for outcomes

Low Self-Confidence

• Thoughts - negative, defeat or failure, doubt

• Feelings - tense, dread, fear. not wanting to take part

• Focus - on others, on less relevant factors (coach,

umpire, conditions)

- Behaviour - lack of effort, likely to give up, unwilling to take risks (rather play safe), blame others or conditions for outcome

Control

Identifying when an athlete feels a particular emotion and understanding the reason for the feelings is an important stage of helping an athlete gain emotional control. An athlete's ability to maintain control of their emotions in the face of adversity and remain positive is essential to successful performance. Two emotions that are often associated with poor performance are anxiety and anger.

Anxiety comes in two forms - Physical (butterflies, sweating, nausea, needing the toilet) and Mental (worry, negative thoughts, confusion, lack of concentration). Relaxation is a technique that can be used to reduce anxiety.

When an athlete becomes angry, the cause of the anger often becomes the focus of attention. This then leads to a lack of concentration on the task, performance deteriorates and confidence in ability is lost which fuels the anger - a slippery slope to failure.

Commitment

Sports performance depends on the athlete being fully committed to numerous goals over many years. In competition with these goals the athlete will have many aspects of daily life to manage. The many competing interests and commitments include work, studies, family/partner, friends, social life and other hobbies/

sports

Within the athlete's sport, commitment can be undermined by:

- a perceived lack of progress or improvement
- not being sufficiently involved in developing the training program
- not understanding the objectives of the training program
- injury
- lack of enjoyment
- anxiety about performance - competition
- becoming bored
- coach athlete not working as a team
- lack of commitment by other athletes

Setting goals with the athlete will raise their feelings of value, give them joint ownership of the goals and therefore become more committed to achieving them. All goals should be SMARTER.

Many people (coach, medical support team, manager, friends, etc.) can contribute to an athlete's levels of commitment with appropriate levels of support and positive feedback, especially during times of injury, illness and poor performance.

Successful Emotional States

The following are emotional states experienced with successful performance:

- H..py - felt that this was my opportunity to demonstrate an excellent performance. Felt I could beat anybody.

• Calm and nervous - Felt nervous but really at ease with these feelings. I accepted and expected to be nervous but felt ready to start.

• Anxious but excited - Felt so ready to compete but a little nervous. Nerves and excitement come together

• Confident - I remembered all the successful training sessions and previous best performances

Psychology Skills Training

Training for the athlete should aim to improve their mental skills, such as self-confidence, motivation, the ability to relax under great pressure, and the ability to concentrate and usually has three phases:

• Education phase, during which athletes learn about the importance of psychological skills and how they affect performance

• Acquisition phase, during which athletes learn about the strategies and techniques to improve the specific psychological skills that they require

• Practice phase, during which athletes develop their psychological skills through repeated practice, simulations, and actual competition.

Thus, it can be said that without knowledge of psychology, no physical educator, coach can provide training to the players properly. Such kind of coach cannot bring the players out of stress which is being created by diverse and complex situations. Only through sports psychology, a coach can prepare the players to face stressful conditions easily and to perform outstandingly even in such conditions.

10

PRINCIPLES AND METHODS OF TEACHING PHYSICAL ACTIVITIES

The main and aim and object of all education is all-round development of individual's personality. To achieve this aim it is very essential for an educational institution or school to provide different activities to its students. Over the years, the educationists have realised to a great extent that the centre of all education is the child or the individual. This implies that the teaching-learning process in education has taken a broader meaning and scope. It is now absurd, if not foolish, to think that teaching is only, passing on the experiences from one generation to the other or that it is merely instruction i.e., do's and do not's of behaviour.

Recent knowledge in the matters of human behaviour has considerably revealed that neither a teacher teaches in isolation nor does a pupil learn in isolation and that the teaching, a process of reciprocal education between the teacher and the taught, is not restricted to the four walls of the school, rather it is very comprehensive and vast. It encompasses the idea that a teacher who does not learn himself, cannot teach at all. A candle that does not burn never lights others. Those who think that they have learnt and there is nothing more for them to learn, have really learnt nothing; they are like blind men grouping in the dark. We talk so much about the balanced personality of the child, the harmonious development of the individual etc., and yet we are quite far from understanding and emphasizing the real meaning of this phase.

Unfortunately, the teaching in schools and colleges is so much bookish and theoretical and formal that it is very difficult if not impossible to come out of this cobweb of undesirable obsession. How can a teacher spare time to understand child when he is yoked like a beast of burden, to books and books only. So teaching the books and just passing on bits of the information is lop-sided education. In fact no teacher can teach unless the child, the beneficiary, is ready to learn or receive. This clearly speaks of the law of readiness in psychology. If teaching is causing to learn, we must admit that teacher is the great source of help to the child who is to understand the nature of things around him.

Education based on bookish knowledge might start after a child is at least three to four years old, the motor skill education starts right from the time of one's birth; whether crawling, toddling, sitting, standing or running with jumpy, unstable steps, it is essentially a part of child behaviour. Later on, these activities form the basis of motor skills, which are utilised as the foundation stones of the complex skills in games and sports. Reading and writing may not be natural activities. Running, jumping, hitting, throwing etc., are basic natural qualities and when used as medium of education need a lot of combination with one another.

Without physical education teacher's and that of the pupil's involvement in the activities, education cannot take place on the play field, in the gymnasium and in the swimming pool. Moreover, movement education requires the use of visual cues to perceive an activity as a whole and the sufficient practice to master that activity. Conditioning or training of certain reflexes is another requirement for mastering some of the fundamental skills. Meaningful practice is the basis of learning in physical education.

LEARNING—AN INTRODUCTORY

Human child goes on adding something to his behaviour through experience right from after his birth. In simple term we might say that he is learning something. The native equipment of learning was already present with the child at birth but now that he has been acquiring such attitudes, skills, habits and mode of walking, talking, thinking etc., he is trying to become the real member of the human society.

This acquisition of modes of behaviour raises him from the state of animalhood to that of humanhood. Because of the highly complex nervous system, the human child has been considered the most educable being on the Earth. In fact, learning is the most comprehensive term encompassing the unhindered process of modification of behaviour through experience which starts at birth and comes to end at death. Maturation and learning go hand in hand because various traits of behaviour appear at various age-levels and many complex skills requires a certain level of maturation. If an individual reacts to a stimulus or a group of stimuli in a different way than he reached last time, we might conclude that he has learnt something.

In the field of physical education, greatest stress is laid on the acquisition and mastering of the motor skills, leading to the learning of very complex skills of games and sports. The end-products of movement education are the health, mental development, social soundness and the skills to utilize the leisure hours in worthwhile ways. In fact, motor skill education is the means through which the mental upliftment and social soundness are ensured. Proper motor skill learning and its practice lead to such behavioural patterns which assist an individual to have all round fitness, economical use of his energies and abilities for the optimal growth and development both physical and mental.

In physical education, the theories and laws of learning propounded by psychologists and physiologists have been quoted extensively and intensively to illustrate the nature of learning. Certain facts which may be interesting to the teacher of physical education are enumerated below:-

(1) Learning is the result of the interaction between human organism and the environment - physical and social.

(2) All activity in physical education is a doing phenomenon and it is essential that emphasis should be put on practice. Repetition and drilling lead to automatization. Only pure insight cannot bring out the desired effect.

(3) Learning is the acquisition of new responses and it inevitably results in progressive changes in the behaviour of the individual.

(4) Learning is an active process and without the involvement of the body and mind - the whole man - new responses cannot be acquired nor can the old and undesirable responses be weakened.

(5) A child would feel immense difficulty in acquiring

a particular response unless he has perceived the act fully and that the concept about the action has engrained itself on his mind.

(6) Learning does not take place in vacuum. It takes place under the circumstances which are favourable and hence surroundings, where there is possibility of the individual to learn some activity, must be reasonably good if not ideal.

(7) Learning is faster where the situation are more life-like because such situations induce the child to learn those responses which are meaningful and useful to him in his life.

(8) Learning is so vastly affected by the hereditary qualities and traits that it has been considered as essentially an individual process.

Learning by Doing

There is really only one way to learn how to do something and that is to do it. If you want to learn to throw a football, drive a car, build a mousetrap, design a building, cook a stir-fry, or be a management consultant, you must have a go at doing it. Throughout history, youths have been apprenticed to masters in order to learn a trade. We understand that learning a skill means eventually trying your hand at the skill. When there is no real harm in simply trying we allow novices to "give it a shot."

Parents usually teach children in this way. They don't give a series of lectures to their children to prepare them to walk, talk, climb, run, play a game, or learn how to behave. They just let their children do these things. We hand a child a ball to teach him to throw. If he throws poorly, he simply tries again.

Parents tolerate sitting in the passenger seat while their teenager tries out the driver's seat for the first time. It's nerve-wracking, but parents put up with it, because they know there's no better way.

According to a great psychologist, movement is the basis of intellectual development besides the physical development. The development of general movement patterns for action is the primary process and lays the foundation for all performances and for all learning. Movement is learning; learning requires movement. He asserts that foundation to every intellectual activity of the human being is the skill of motor control and coordination. Thoughts which do not get into muscles never fully possess the mind. One can understand by such observation that all learning phenomena converge on movement i.e., doing. Without the individual's involvement in the activity, it is not possible for him to grasp and master that activity.

The concept of learning by doing has spread far and wide and every where it is being emphasised that children must involve themselves in activities, rather than act as passive listeners or spectators. In physical education, learning by doing is fundamental to all activities of games and sports.

No one has ever acquired skills of games and sports without having done and practised them. Kicking, jumping, throwing, running, which constitute the plinth of physical education are not learnt from books but through practice which is purposeful and in line with the natural behaviour of the individual. Doing and practising strengthen the link between the stimulus and the response while passivity weakens it.

Innumerable studies have been conducted to show

that learning by doing is much superior, efficient and ever lasting and yet there is no agreement on the question of how much doing or practice is required. However, certain findings with regard to the fundamental skills in games and sports and the duration of their practice for better coordination and performance may be of greater interest to the teachers of physical education.

(1) Motor-skill learning is a practical training and needs comparatively less theorizing. Those who are in the habit of lecturing too much on the playfield, make teaching learning process a bad affair. Children must be initiated into the activity right at the outset.

(2) Practice periods, during the learning stage, should be planned keeping in view the ultimate objective of the activity.

(3) Efficiency of an individual in any particular skill depends on how much it has been practised or repeated with accurate procedure and precision.

(4) In the absence of elimination of mistakes in the beginning or at the right time, the practice of motor skills and fundamentals of a game will certainly be futile and lead to nowhere. Rather it would be very difficult afterwards to rectify the wrong pattern adopted by the children.

(5) Regularity is the hall-mark of practice, and that is why it should be perennial though scheduled according to the seasons. In no case, should practice be discontinued.

Besides all this, the modern educators in education have now confirmed that the child's participation in any activity is a must and from this point of view physical education is an ideal field of practical training in life. Apart from the physical benefits, the virtues which one requires to become an acceptable member of the human society are not the result of precept on the play field but they are the living products of those practical experiences which a child lives through.

Motivation as a Instrument to Learning

Motivation is the set of reasons that determines one to engage in a particular behaviour. The term is generally used for human motivation but, theoretically, it can be used to describe the causes for animal behaviour as well. According to various theories, motivation may be rooted in the basic need to minimize physical pain and maximize pleasure, or it may include specific needs such as eating and resting, or a desired object, hobby, goal, state of being, ideal, or it may be attributed to less-apparent reasons such as altruism, morality, or avoiding mortality. Motivation is the process by which an individual is inspired to learn or to do an activity. It is one of the most important conditions rather the central core of learning; it is a psycho-physiological condition which causes one to work or strive to fulfil his needs. In fact, to motivate a child is to induce him to move—mentally and/or bodily. Learning becomes an uphill task if there is no whole hearted participation on the part of the learner. Interest, desire, need, incentives, pressures, tension etc., affect the process of motivation. Psychologists have claimed and it is very true that an individual would never learn unless he is ready to learn or has been prepared to do so.

Motives, when aroused, trigger off drives in the individual who seeks the fulfilment of his desires which have been fermented in him. There is so much of felt-need in the individual to learn that he goes on learning without any pressure from outside – a sort of automatic behaviour, in which teacher serves as a guide and not as a dictator or a director. Motivation brings in easiness, satisfaction and contentment in learning. In physical education, a teacher may motivate the child by two ways viz., by intrinsic or subjective methods and extrinsic or objective methods to stimulate learning, with the use of rewards, awards, certificates, marks, badges etc. However, educationists have agreed that the intrinsic motivation is more valuable since it brings durable and lasting modifications in the behaviour of the child, while the extrinsic motivation is less natural because in such case, the child there concentrates more on procuring certification for his performance than the joy of activity.

MOTIVATIONAL THEORIES

Drive Reduction Theories

Drive theory

There are a number of drive theories. The Drive Reduction Theory grows out of the concept that we have certain biological needs, such as hunger. As time passes the strength of the drive increases as it is not satisfied. Then as we satisfy that drive by fulfilling its desire, such as eating, the drive's strength is reduced. It is based on the theories of Freud and the idea of feedback control systems, such as a thermostat.

There are several problems, however, that leave the validity of the Drive Reduction Theory open for debate. The first problem is that it does not explain how Secondary Reinforcers reduce drive. For example, money does not satisfy any biological or psychological need but reduces drive on a regular basis through a pay check second-order conditioning. Secondly, if the drive reduction theory held true we would not be able to explain how a hungry human being can prepare a meal without eating the food before they finished cooking it.

However, when comparing this to a real life situation such as preparing food, one does get hungrier as the food is being made (drive increases), and after the food has been consumed the drive decreases. The only reason the food does not get eaten before is the human element of restraint and has nothing to do with drive theory. Also, the food will either be nicer after it is cooked, or it won't be edible at all before it is cooked.

PRINCIPLES OF TEACHING

Teaching is considered to be a specialised field like other professional fields i.e., medical, legal, fashion designing, film industry etc. Teaching is the result of laborious and painstaking effort; it is considered as an art through the ages.

From the point of view of teaching, each teacher is a separate entity and he differs from other teachers significantly; during the course of time each teacher discovers and adopts his own ways, techniques, methods of teaching, etc., which give him a characteristic distinction. Hence a teacher may, at least in the modern set of circumstances, not be expected to treat the old path or follow the technique handed down to him conventially. Yet there are certain fundamental maxims which the teacher is expected to follow. These maxims are as follows: -

(1) Make the Goal Clear

Mostly children are unaware from the objective of the activity or they often do not know that why they are learning the activity or why they are being taught the activity; simply learning for the sake of learning leads the pupil no where. Generally half-hearted participation is more harmful than no participation.

(2) Constant Evaluation is the watch-word of modern education

Evaluation involves judgement by the teachers and pupils to determine progress made in the programme of the physical activities. It is not difficult in physical education to ascertain the level of one's performance and the impact of teacher's instruction, or guidance. Evaluation is the spur to progress and future planning. This helps the teacher to know whether his teaching has been fruitful or not, and to eliminate the undesirable element from his techniques and activities from the programme of physical education.

(3) Keeping up your interest and that of pupils in the activity

We generally do what interests us and perhaps repeat it again and again. Interest is one of the basic factors in learning and teaching. A teacher will never teach unless it interests him to teach. Nor will the pupil learn in the absence of his interest in the activity. Interest is the motivating force, it provides the drive to engage in an activity, insures rapid learning and provides satisfying experience. When children lose interest, they avoid activity.

(4) Make yourself familiar with the general age characteristics of your pupils

A physical education teacher handling a class in the primary section of education is confronted with different problems that the one coaching a college team simply because the pupils at both the level of education have entirely different characteristics of behaviour. Modification of behaviour is greatly affected by the maturity level of children.

(5) Proceed from simple to complex, concrete to abstract, known to unknown

Simple motor skills as running, walking, jumping, hitting, kicking etc., are the foundations of the complex fundamental skills of all the competitive games and sports. Children need sufficient mastery over the motor skills before taking to complex sports. The teacher of physical education should base his programmes on the principle of progression, i.e., he should start according to the age group with the primary things first and then gradually proceed to teach complexities of the activity. In the beginning the physical activities must be in the form of play based on concrete ideas involving concrete material.

(6) Let there be a blend of the formal and the informal

Generally rigid systems of physical education lay stress upon formal techniques of teaching. But there is now more of effort on the part of the planners to informalise education i.e., to give more and more opportunity of freedom of action to the pupils so that their dependence upon the teachers is minimized yet it is undesirable to do away with the formal teaching wholly.

(7) Avoid being rigid

Rigidity in planning, stiffness in implementation in following norms and standards make teaching a dull affair whereas higher accomplishment can be had by allowing flexibility at all levels of teaching-learning process. Planning with regard to organisation, choice of activities, methods and techniques of teaching needs to be flexible and adaptive because of the pupil's differences in genetic endowment, growth and development levels, maturity, environmental background, knowledge, skill, previous experience etc.

(8) Essence of Recreation

The physical education teacher should have good sense of humour. He should not always be strict with his pupils and provide them bookish knowledge all the time in the class room teaching rather than he should extend his teaching to the sport activities, games, drill, marching and recreational activities so that the pupils may feel refresh and give attention and interest to their teacher's teachings.

(9) From Analysis to Synthesis

It is generally accepted that every individual has the ability to accept, understand, compare and analyse the problem with its different aspects, with its help a person tries to synthesize the problem. This very synthesis is the process of learning with the help of the study process, the teacher keeps the analysis of the different principles of study in front of the students.

(10) From Indefinite to Definite

There is a common experience in the study of science that mentally the student is in a state of doubt when the experiments, observations or principles and taught but when he performs the same thing in the laboratory and finds that what he has learnt is similar to what he is doing then the doubt from the mind comes to an end.

TEACHING METHODS—MEANING AND SCOPE

Teaching is considered as an art which encompasses not only the good classroom sittings and lengthy and tidy discussion but it is consisted of all those situations in which the educator comes into contact with the students any where across the world. In the field of physical education, a teacher or instructor has to perform multifarious responsibilities viz., he has to teach his pupils some skills; he has to supervises some others; he has to give coaching to the athletes, he has to conduct the competitions and so on; he performs all these activities in order to achieve the higher accomplishments.

All the spheres of education is generally concerned with learning; the process of modification of the behaviour of an individual through experience. Usually an individual learn himself without any help in order to be an acceptable member of the society, this is one of the modes of the human behaviour. While some of the modes of behaviour are to be achieved during one's life time while much of the innate and unlearnt behaviour is to be modified.

The older generation helps the younger generation in the acquisition of new responses and this is the basis of teacher-learning process in the educational institutions. No teaching can be possible without the essence of learning on the part of the disciples or pupils. In other words, we can say that teaching and learning are inter-related and inseparable. Though they are not synonymous yet without one the other is meaningless and worthless.

It is believed by educators that student teaching is one of the most important aspects of the professional preparation of teachers. Those responsible for designing the student-teaching program must remember that the experiences of the student teacher should be a series of activities as nearly like the real teaching situation as possible.

In physical education, the teacher usually adopt a method which decidedly has far reaching effects on the learning of his students due to the complexity of the task involved in the field of physical education which is a wonderful confluence of theory and practice. It is due to defective and inefficient methods and techniques that many a teacher usually failed to deliver the good to his pupils.

Generally, a skilful teacher is easily distinguishable from the one who is unskilled. Moreover, no one can easily learn and apply the skill so easily as it is the result of long years of industry, patience, endurance and experience.

Through many and varied experiences, opportunities should be provided for physical education student teachers to develop the ability:

1. To motivate pupils to develop and maintain good health and physical fitness;

2. To guide learners in the pursuit of knowledge and skills;

3. To prepare boys and girls to become socially competent and worthwhile citizens; and

4. To prepare pupils to assume their responsibilities in a democratic society.

It is generally recognized in the profession that there is great significant in the student-teaching experience as part of teacher preparation. Student teaching is a basic requirement for state certification and a principal prerequisite for the approval of an institution by the

National Council for the Accreditation of Teacher Education.

Student teaching is the time when the student tests the knowledge and techniques he has learned in professional courses in the light of their practically, feasibility, and effectiveness in a particular situation.

This is the time that the student teacher puts into practice theories of education, along with his own ideas, so that he becomes skilled, and ready for a full-time teaching position. Since it is a time for the student teacher to practice, some educators refer to this experience as "practice teaching".

In order for the student-teaching experience to be productive and worthwhile, it is essential to have the cooperation of three people:

1. The supervising teacher, who is a regular teacher of physical education in the school and who has been delegated by the school to supervise the student teacher;

2. The college supervisor, who represents the college or university and assigns and prejudicially supervises student teachers in schools; and

3. The student teacher, the focal point of both the college supervisor and the supervising teacher.

He has a dual responsibility, in that he is a student at the college or university and he is teaching pupils in a school.

For children to reach their full potential in our schools, it would seem to be essential that teachers engage in effective teaching practices. Classroom based investigation has been able to determine effective research-based teaching practices that are related to positive learning outcomes. This understanding has led to the use of the term effective teaching.

The majority of the research on effective teaching has been conducted in the classroom environment, concentrating on more traditional subject areas such as mathematics and language arts. A relatively small amount of information has been gathered in the area of physical education. Consequently, knowledge of what is effective teaching in physical education and how it supports student-learning outcomes is relatively thin, with only a small number of studies providing insight. It is a research gap that needs to be attended to if teachers of physical education are to truly understand how to support student learning by effective teaching.

Related Literature

In recent years, there has been considerable interest in the identification of teaching skills and competencies. The monitoring of standards and the quality of teaching performance has become most apparent in public schools. The notion of being an effective teacher is an important and a critical goal for educators if they are to become better at what they do and if a knowledge base is to be developed in order to train and educate those teachers entering the profession. Although effective teaching is a term that can be difficult to define in a precise manner, it can be argued, that teachers are viewed as effective in their teaching when students achieve intended learning outcomes.

EFFECTIVE TEACHING

Classroom Research

Although teaching has been a focus of attention for many years, research on teaching is still a relatively new field of inquiry. Initially, studies tended to be focused on teachers, not on the learning environment, trying to identify characteristics or qualities of effective teachers. For example, the initial idea of an effective teacher in the early 1900s was a judgement primarily based on the "goodness" of a person. Honesty, generosity, friendliness, dedication, and consideration were all regarded to be vital components of an effective teacher. These personal qualities needed to be demonstrated in an authoritarian, disciplined, and organized classroom. Unfortunately, this definition of an effective teacher lacked any objective standards of performance.

It was not until the 1960s that there was a shift in the focus from the personal characteristics of teachers to teacher and student behaviours. For the first time, researchers began to visit classrooms to gather information, specifically to study teacher and student interactions. Instruments were developed to measure classroom interactions: frequency of interaction, types of questions, and response rates. These instruments were employed in research studies in the belief that effective teaching behaviours could be identified and, once identified, could be taught to teachers.

During the 1980s, research tried to identify the facets of classroom teaching that promoted an effective learning environment for children. Much of what we do know about effective teaching comes from this research base. These well-conducted classroom research studies attempted to identify what teachers do to produce student learning.

In a review of research studies that showed an impact on student achievement and learning, Borich summarized effective teaching methods and outlined five key teaching behaviours that were supported by research: lesson clarity; instructional variety; teacher task orientation; engagement in the learning process; and student success rate. Borich also found that five other behaviours seem to be related to effective teaching. He identified this second group of teaching behaviours as helping behaviours. However, the research identifying these helping behaviours is not as extensive as the research support for the original five key behaviours, and so the findings are not as conclusive. Nevertheless, using student ideas and contributions, structuring, questioning, probing, and teacher affect have been identified as additional behaviours that act as a catalyst to enhance the performance of the five key behaviours.

Research on Teaching in Physical Education

As the majority of the research on effective teaching has been concentrated in traditional academic subject areas such as mathematics and language arts, physical educators were left to develop their own parallel research studies that were specific to their context. Hence, compared to most school subjects, physical education was a late arrival on the teacher effectiveness scene. The major research studies involving effectiveness in physical education have studied such areas as student engagement, curriculum time allocation, teaching methods, teacher behaviour, and teacher perceptions, but have not applied the classroom research findings identified by researchers such as Borich.

With regard to effective teaching in the realm of physical education, studies indicate that 3 many teachers believe they are teaching effectively. This conclusion is based primarily on the teacher's own perception of important teaching criteria: such as explanation, feedback, demonstration, and student enjoyment. According to Siedentop, for the most part, these perceptions could be considered accurate. Teachers do include explanation, feedback, and demonstration in their lessons, and students do enjoy classes. However, it could be suggested, from the definitions of effective teaching provided by Berliner, Brophy, Gage, Harris and Rosenshine, that such teacher perceptions are not accurate measures of effectiveness since student learning is not considered.

It would seem that if student learning is a goal of teaching, then teachers should view student learning as being of prime importance. However, in the area of physical education, there is research evidence to suggest that this is not necessarily the case.

Placek investigated teacher planning in physical education. She noted that student behaviour and environmental unpredictability had the greatest impact on a teacher's planning. Placek noted that successful physical education teaching was often defined by the teachers as keeping students participating (busy), with minimal misbehaviour (good), while providing enjoyment (happy). Placek concluded that the teachers were more concerned about student behaviour than the transmission of knowledge. In an attempt to further understand physical education teaching, Placek investigated student teachers' perceptions of successful and unsuccessful physical education teaching. Similar to experienced teachers, Placek reported that student teachers regarded successful teaching when their students were being busy, happy, and good.

Schempp, in studying the transformation from student teacher to teacher, found that student teachers rated physical education activities that were teacher approved as being very important. However, it was not the activity that was of key importance, but student engagement in the activity. In analyzing student teaching, Schempp noted that keeping students busy was of prime importance for student teachers when teaching physical education. Student teachers were satisfied when students were working (busy), enjoying themselves (happy), and were responding with questions and doing as they were told (good).

Borys and Fishburne replicated Placek's research in a Canadian university setting with high school preservice teachers. Their findings supported the conclusions drawn by Placek. Student teachers conceive successful physical education teaching not to be related to student learning but rather in keeping students busy, happy, and good. In gathering further information on successful physical education teaching, Fishburne and Borys compared the conceptions of elementary school preservice teachers with those of experienced elementary school teachers. Once again, learning was not found to be the prime goal associated with successful teaching. Hickson and Fishburne in a study comparing elementary school preservice teachers' and experienced elementary school teachers' perceptions of successful physical education teaching compared to other curriculum areas, found that in physical education teaching the trend of busy, happy, and good was evident for both student teachers and experienced teachers, with student learning receiving a low priority. However, when considering successful teaching in other curriculum areas, both student teachers and experienced teachers, rated student learning as the highest indicator of successful teaching.

The research findings of these studies suggest that both student teachers and experienced teachers regard successful teaching of physical education differently from the definitions of effective teaching provided by Berliner, Brophy, Gage, Harris and Rosenshine.

CHARACTERISTICS OF EFFECTIVE PHYSICAL EDUCATION TEACHING

In a review of physical education teaching research, Silverman suggested the following characteristics for the effective teaching of motor skills: the planning for class management and student learning; the anticipation of situations and contingency plans; the awareness of individual student skill differences and use of such information in planning and monitoring; the acquisition of information to plan; the knowledge of, and when to use, a repertoire of teaching styles; the accuracy and focus of explanation and demonstration; the provision for adequate student practice time; the maximization of appropriate student practice and engagement; the minimization of inappropriate student practice and engagement; and the minimization of pupil waiting.

However, Silverman's review has come under criticism by researchers. For example, one of the criticisms from Dodds and Placek was that the "...list also focuses on what teachers do, ignoring both the specific student outcomes that accrue as a result and intended teacher goals relevant to a given teaching situation".

Rink also reviewed the research on effective teaching and identified seven distinct teacher characteristics associated with effective instruction in the physical education realm. She identified the following teacher characteristics: the identification of intended outcomes for learning; the planning of learning experiences to accomplish these outcomes; the presentation of tasks in a clear manner; the organization and management of the learning environment; the monitoring of the environment; the development of the lesson content based on student responses; and the evaluation of the effectiveness of instructional/curricular process.

Mawer in a review of research and viewpoints on effective teaching of physical education, suggested that the following characteristics are indicative of effective teaching: the planning of work effectively; the good presentation of new material; the organization and management of the learning experiences and students; the active involvement of the teacher in teaching students; the provision of a supportive and positive learning environment; the acquisition of a repertoire of teaching styles; and the ability to teach for the facilitation of student understanding of concepts and lesson content.

The characteristics suggested by Silverman, Rink and Mawer bear some similarity to Borich's work. Several factors such as lesson clarity, structure, involving student ideas, and instructional variety have a commonality among the lists. However, there seems to be little, if any, research that has directly looked at the suggested characteristics of effective teachers from the research reviews of Silverman, Mawer, Rink or Borich to determine if the identified characteristics actually do affect student learning in the physical education domain.

The purpose of the present study was to gain an understanding of what is effective teaching in physical education. This is a research gap that needs to be attended to if teachers of physical education are to truly understand how to support student learning. Therefore, this research study examined the effectiveness of a teacher development program on teacher behaviour and, ultimately, the student-learning environment in a physical education setting.

Research Design

The research study utilized two methods of data gathering. A single-case, multiple baseline design was employed to determine the effectiveness of the teacher development program intervention strategy and interviews were conducted in order to understand the teachers' opinions of the teacher development program and their teaching and also to understand the students' opinions of their physical education lessons.

The independent variable in this study was a teacher development program. The program was developed from the conclusions drawn from classroom research and from the opinions of physical education researchers about effective teaching characteristics. The dependent variables in this study were the student behaviours that have been identified by researchers as being important determinants of lesson effectiveness for student learning. These variables were the amount of lesson time that students spent: waiting; in transition; in management activity; in inappropriate activity; receiving information; in engaged activity, and in off-task activity. Student behavioural data were collected through the use of a systematic observation system, Duration Recording. Teacher opinions of the teacher development program were collected through personal interviews. Similarly, student data were also collected through interviews in order to understand their opinions of their physical education lessons.

Participants

Three generalist trained elementary school teachers from the same elementary school were selected for this research study. The selection of the three teachers was based upon their declared personal interest in participating in the research study. All three teachers were female and their years of teaching experience ranged from three to nineteen years. Teacher A was a female, grade 4/5 teacher with 25 students in her class, Teacher B taught a grade 2 class with 22 students, and Teacher C taught 24 students in her grade 1 class. Students were also considered as participants within the research study. Six students from each of the three classes were randomly chosen to provide information concerning their opinions of their physical education lessons.

The Teacher Development Program

Each teacher participated in a teacher development program. The program was introduced to the teachers in the form of a professional development program. A total of 5.5 hours of individual sessions was provided to each teacher. All three teachers received the same topics in the same set order.

Topic #1 - The role of physical education for children. This topic area investigated the role of physical education. In particular, the aims and goals of a quality physical education program were discussed, together with the importance of physical education in the overall educational experience of children. A critical component of this topic was the development of the participant's knowledge and understanding of the value of physical education. Issues such as health and fitness, growth and development, active lifestyle, skill development, personal and social development, self-confidence and self-esteem, and goal setting were addressed in order to for the participant to understand the qualities and the benefits of a quality physical education program. Participants were exposed to research findings that support the inclusion of physical education in the overall educational experiences of children to illustrate the value of physical education in the holistic development of students.

Topic #2 - The importance and understanding of developmental appropriateness. In this topic, information was presented and discussed to enhance an understanding of what developmental appropriateness is in a physical education setting, what constitutes a developmentally appropriate program, and how such a program can be designed by a teacher to meet the developmental needs of the children in his/her class. In particular, the following were covered: (a) what a developmentally appropriate physical education program consists of ; (b) what programs need to be and how they can be taught in order to recognize the unique needs of the individual based on his/her cognitive, emotional and social, and physical needs; (c) what the three developmental levels commonly found in elementary school settings are (Developmental Level I - Kindergarten to Grade 2, Developmental Level II - Grades 3 and 4, Developmental Level III - Grades 5 and 6); (d) what the characteristics are that children at these levels exhibit; (e) what the particular learning requirements children in these levels have, and (f) what teaching considerations are required to support learning opportunities at each developmental level.

Topic #3 - Putting theory into practice. The third topic in the teacher development program considered the issue of taking the theoretical information identified in the review of related literature and placing it into the day-to-day practice of teaching. This topic introduced the research work of Borich and the reviews conducted by Silverman, Rink, and Mawer in order to develop a knowledge of the identified effective teaching behaviours and characteristics of teachers, and how this knowledge can be incorporated into regular teaching practice in physical education lessons. The teacher participants were engaged in discussion about how and why each of the identified teaching characteristics is essential for effective teaching. For example, behaviours such as planning were discussed as it is identified as an effective teaching behaviour.

Topic #4 - Effective teaching. The importance of student learning in physical education was stressed in this topic. The research work of Placek, Schempp, and Hickson and Fishburne were presented and discussed. Ideas for planning for student learning were explored and developed. In particular, the notion of Busy, Happy, and Good was discussed in regard to the issues that make a lesson effective. The effective teaching strategies/ techniques presented in the previous session were considered in regards to personal teaching habits.

Topic #5 - Instructional strategy. This topic aimed to develop an understanding of what a teacher can do to improve his/her instructional strategy. The understanding and selection of teaching styles and methods that are most effective in physical education settings were explored, as was the importance of student engagement, and management of the learning environment. Participants were introduced to the factors that influence the choice of teaching style and method, for example the learning outcome aimed for, the needs of the learner, the lesson content, and the environment. Also, different teaching strategies were considered. For example, the effectiveness of station work when limited equipment is available, the use of task cards to focus student attention and learning and to minimize time students spent receiving instructions.

Topic #6 - The effective teaching model, the theoretical framework, and its implementation. The effective teaching model, designed specifically for this study, was introduced in this topic. The model was developed from the review of related research to provide a focus for the teacher development program. The model incorporated the teacher characteristics that are associated with effective instruction in physical education. The model consisted of three distinct phases: a thought and planning phase, a decision-making and action phase, and a reflection phase. The structure and content of the teaching model is illustrated in Figure 1. The three-phase model was explained and discussed so the participant understood the various components associated with the model and the theoretical framework upon which it is based. The three phases were discussed and attention was drawn to important features. For example in Phase I, the thought and planning phase of the model, the teacher needs to consider two important features: the determination of student needs and the planning for student learning. This requires the teacher to decide upon the needs of the students in the class with regard to the choice of activity, the developmental appropriateness of the activity, and the curricular relevance and when planning for student learning to determine exactly what is the learning outcome for the lesson and how it might best be achieved. It was discussed why this phase would occur prior to the lesson being taught and comparisons were made between the present practice of the teacher participant and what was aimed for.

In Phase II, the decision-making and action phase of the model considers what needs to occur during the lesson. It was explained that the teacher needed to consistently consider and assess what is occurring in the lesson and how it serves the learning needs of the students. Teaching style and method, clarity of presentation, the provision of positive and well-managed environment in order to support and optimize the learning situation, and the need to ensure that there is a high level of student engagement were all brought to the teacher's attention importance discussed. Phase III of the model consists post-lesson reflection and the evaluation of effectiveness.

Topic #7 - The importance of reflection. This topic considered the importance of post-lesson reflection and the evaluation of lesson effectiveness. Understanding that teacher development requires observation, analysis, and judgment about what occurs during instruction and using that information to make changes in personal teaching behaviours was a critical feature of this topic. The participant explored ways to reflect upon her teaching performance and student learning, and also developed an understanding of how to evaluate for effectiveness. To create relevance and a connection to the teacher participants present practice, reference was made to evaluation and reflection behaviours that they already practiced in other curricula areas.

11

EVALUATION PROCESSES AND TECHNIQUES

Why a New Evaluation Process?

Evaluations establish opportunities for organisational learning and for the improvement of policies, programmes and projects in the light of experience. But they do not automatically ensure that our partners will learn from these lessons, nor that IFAD policies, programmes or projects will be re-oriented. This is the responsibility of the Partnership: PMD staff, Borrower, CBOs and other stakeholders. We can, however, design an evaluation process that forges a stronger link between learning lessons and implementing them.

The importance of learning to the evaluation process has always been evident, but what is becoming increasingly clear is that those who are expected to use evaluation recommendations and lessons for improving performance should participate in the process of developing these recommendations. Our partners both act and reflect on their actions. Certainly an objective external point of view may be valuable to the learning process, however, the performance of operations will be enhanced by the degree to which OE's partners entrusted with the implementation of operations become the motivated learners, and are able to translate into action what they have learned through evaluation work. To be effective, our evaluation processes need to respond to this requirement.

To drive learning towards action, we are introducing three main features to the New Evaluation Process (NEP):

The Approach Paper as the starting point of each evaluation;

The concept of Core Learning Partnership to steer the evaluation process; and

The definition of the completion point of each evaluation process as an agreement or understanding among OE and its partner

One of the most important features of this process is the agreement from the outset on a completion point for the evaluation, which will bring the main actors together to identify and agree upon the key issues to be analysed. This will consequently lead to the formulation of lessons learned and recommendations that are most appropriate for performance improvement. The NEP also requires OE's evaluation partners to anticipate how they will use the recommendations at the end of the process. This results-oriented approach assures that the NEP will respond to the needs of the partnership.

In addition, the NEP will experiment with the use of Core Learning Partnerships (CLPs) composed of core partners that will steer the evaluation process throughout its cycle. The CLP is an informal and flexible platform for partnership, open deliberations and learning among the key stakeholders. It can range from a group of stakeholders who are consulted at various steps in the process to a clearly identified core of partners with whom we collaborate to manage the evaluation learning process. The CLP may be organised for a variety of reasons: to develop an evaluation action plan; design the stakeholder participation approach; collaborate on the design of the Approach Paper; discuss progress of the evaluation efforts; discuss findings, conclusions and recommendations, and finally, to organise the negotiations and agreements about lessons learned and recommendations and next steps to take in implementation. Although the OE team is responsible for the integrity of the final outcome of the evaluation analysis, by engaging the CLP in guiding the learning process, OE intends to increase the commitment of our evaluation partners to the final outcome of the evaluation process. The CLP will serve as a platform on effective and real time transfer of knowledge and learning generated through evaluation to design and operation.

The Approach Paper is a new instrument for OE. We have always used highly detailed Terms of Reference to guide past evaluation missions, however, the Approach Paper goes beyond this. It describes the overall framework for the evaluation, describes the process that the CLP will use throughout and the kinds of methods it might employ during each step, and finally, defines the expected results.

OE will also endeavour to keep its evaluation processes as short as feasible, while preserving analytical rigour as well as allowing enough time for discussion and interaction with all partners to stimulate joint learning. In 2000 OE will endeavour to keep the time involved between the drafting of the Approach Paper (Step 2) and the Completion Point (Step 6) within the following indicative deadlines:

Physical Education Tests

It is not within the scope of this chapter to outline

test procedures for every test in physical education. The following list of tests includes examples of those being used successfully to assess the various aspects of physical education.

Rogers Strength Test

This test includes seven items—right and left grip strength, back lift, leg lift, push-ups, pull-ups, and lung capacity. The gross score is a measure of overall strength called the strength index. The physical Fitness Index is obtained by dividing the strength index by the norm.

Kraus-Waber Test

This is a test of minimum muscular fitness and consists of six items each testing the strength of a specific muscle group; or the flexibility of the body.

Cable-Tension Strength Tests

A tensiometer that measures the tension on a cable is the principal instrument. Tests have been devised to measure the strength of approximately forty different muscle groups throughout the body.

Larson Strength Test

The items consist of chins, dips, and the vertical jump. It is useful for classifying and grouping students.

New York State Physical Fitness Test

Posture, throwing accuracy, strength, agility, speed, balance, and endurance are measured. The test is designed to provide an instrument with which to evaluate the status and progress in fitness of boys and girls grades four to twelve.

Army Physical Efficiency Test

The items are pull-ups, squat jumps, push-ups, sit-ups, and 300-yard shuttle run. It is used to test the physical condition of members of the armed forces.

Tuttle Pulse-Ratio Test

Subjects step up and down on a 13-inch stool. A formula using the resting pulse rate and the pulse rate after exercise has been devised. The test score is based on the ability of the heart to compensate for exercise.

Harvard Step Test

Subjects step up and down on a 20-inch bench the rate of 30 steps per minute for five minutes. The duration of the exercise in seconds × 100, divided by 2 × the sum of pulse counts in recovery gives the score. It is one of the best of the tests measuring cardiovascular endurance.

Wetzel Grid

This is a chart that depicts the growth and development of the individual based on measures of age, height, and weight. It provides a cumulative growth record during the child's school years and in most cases detects serious deviations from accepted norms.

General Motor Capacity

This test, developed by McCloy, is intended to measure an individual's innate potential. The score is obtained by combining the results of the Classification Index, the Sergeant Jump, the low Brace Text, and the Burpee Test.

The Johnson Test

Classified as a test of motor educability, the Johanson Test consists of a number of balancing and hopping stunts performed on a mat.

The Sargent Jump

This consists of leaping vertically as high as possible. There are a number of adaptations. Basically, it measures the ability of the extensor muscles to "explode" and generate force and velocity.

Aerobic Capacity

Most physiologists accept the measurement of maximal oxygen consumption as the most valid test of cardiorespiratory fitness. There are three general methods of measurement—treadmill running, riding the bicycle radiometer, and stepping up and down on a bench. There are carefully prescribed directions that must be followed for accurate measurement.

Scott Motor Ability Battery

The three items contained in this test are the obstacle course, the basketball throw for distance, and the standing broad jump. It was designed to be used for testing high school and college women but has also been modified by Kilday and Latchaw to measure motor ability in ninth-grade boys.

Achievement Tests

These are tests to measure the performance of students in skills taught in physical education classes. There are now available achievement tests for most of the skills commonly taught. By administering tests at various time intervals, the improvement of the students can be assessed. Teachers may use previously validated and scientifically constructed tests, or they may devise tests of their own.

Tests of Knowledge and Understanding

Written tests of knowledge and understanding in physical education are similar in format to those in other subjects. All teachers and supervisors will be familiar with their preparation and grading.

Other Evaluative Processes

While the assessment of changes in pupils is the ultimate criterion by which the success of a program should be measured, there are many other evaluation devices that will assist in Keeping the administration informed. Some of these are :

Medical and Health Records

These should be kept meticulously. Form time to time, they should be studied scientifically be qualified research specialists and the findings interpreted for practical application.

Student Checklists

Students set goals for themselves, write them down in a notebook, and check them off as they are achieved. Checklists of stunts to perform, records to attain, teams to make, mountains to climb, weights to lift, or deeds to do can be helpful and inspiring. They also reveal students' progress.

Critical Incidents

Teachers and supervisors may employ the critical incident technique to evaluate the behaviour of pupils. A record of incidents will reveal good and bad behaviour and progress toward a higher level.

Questionnaires and Surveys

These may be utilized to assess attitudes toward physical education, interests, and suggestions for future programs. Successive questionnaires a year or more apart may reveal changes in attitudes and accomplishments.

Cumulative Records

Cumulative personnel records will reveal a child's adjustment to school, physical condition, test scores, grades in school, abscnces due to illness, intelligence scores, and many other useful bits of information indicating progress or lack of it.

Autobiographies

Some teachers find an autobiography or a statement of the student's philosophy of life very helpful in understanding his/her motivation, ambitions, and problems.

Sociometric Techniques

Sociograms, social Distance Scales, and similar techniques are helpful in determining the student's relationship with others, status with peers, and how he/she behaves in a group.

Daily Schedules

Students who keep diaries or other personal inventories can learn much about themselves through this practice. If the diaries are kept with the understanding that they may be reviewed periodically be the teacher, they will probably not reveal much of the students' inner thinking, but they can still include a great deal of information about their habits, friends, recreation, and social life.

Anecdotal Records

The pupil, the teacher, or both they keep anecdotal records. If these are carefully kept and not cluttered up with too many trivial note, they can be a valuable source of information.

Rating Scales

Rating scales are widely used to evaluate individuals,

courses, and programs. They identify judgments about the degree to which qualities and characteristics are present. They make possible the combining of the judgment of many people in assessing the quality of facilities, teaching, administering, and performing. They are a necessary adjunct to evaluation at all levels.

The Administrator and Evaluation

While pupil growth and progress are the basic criteria upon which to judge the success of any educational enterprise, administrators need to be kept informed about many other phases of the operation for which they are responsible. Evaluation of the teaching, the environment, the staff work, the facilities, the supervision, the fiscal procedures, the coaching, and the administration itself are important. Some of the means of being kept informed are:

Personnel Audits

These are usually written evaluations of teachers, secretaries, custodians, and other personnel. They may be in the form of written memorandums or standardized rating sheets. Any individual who has supervisory responsibilities should be required to turn in periodically a completed evaluation form describing the competence with which those under his or her jurisdiction have performed. While these are always requested at the time recommendations for salary increments and promotions are being considered, they may also be submitted more frequently.

Such personnel audits should provide the superior with as many specifics as possible. Too often they take the form of vague generalities that are not very meaningful and do little to substantiate the recommendations for tenure, promotion, salary increases, and the like.

Equipment and Facility Checks

Custodians, teachers, and other personnel should be required to submit reports of safety hazards of every description. Unsafe playground equipment, fire hazards, slippery floors, broken bleacher seats, open manholes, worn-out bolts or chains, unguarded trenches or ditches, traffic hazards, or reckless behaviour—all should be reported. There should be immediate follow-up to see that remedial action is taken.

Observation

Regardless of the formal and scheduled evaluation processes, which are part of the normal operation, careful attention should be paid to what is seen, heard, and sensed. An experienced and sensitive administrator does not need to move about in the department very long or converse with very many staff members before being able to assess the climate. The warmth or lack of it as the department head enters the offices of staff members, the spirit of buoyancy or of depression, the exhibition of anxiety or of relaxation, and the openness or restraint that characterizes the conversation—all these are easily discernable and quite informative.

An administrator is constantly evaluating. Whether talking to a pupil reading the school paper, attending a basketball game, or walking through a crowded hallway, one is listening, observing, sensing. In meetings with staff members, either individually or in groups, in reviewing budget requests, signing requisitions, reading memorandums, participating in coffee breaks, or playing a game of golf, the administrator is assimilating and evaluating.

Reports

Annual, quarterly, special, and other types of reports may be required by various administrative officers. These constitute one way of keeping informed but should not be the only means employed. Even such written reports must be carefully interpreted. There are many instances where a written report represents a program in glowing terms—yet a deeper investigation reveals weaknesses and flaws.

Supervision and Evaluation

These two processes bear a very close relationship. Both serve the same basic purpose—as efforts to make the outcomes coincide with the aims and objectives. Both processes proceed continuously; both employ informal and formal procedures; both are applied to all aspects of the operation. Supervision, however, is more concerned with remedial action while evaluation is concerned principally with assessment and appraisal.

Physical Education Evaluation—Appraisals

The determination and appraisal of what has happened or what is happening to boys and girls as a result of school experiences is known as evaluation. Evaluation is important in the modern school as a means of discovering the points at which individual pupils need assistance. It is also important as a means of discovering the effectiveness of the physical education programme as a whole. Unfortunately, we think of testing as a basis for grading pupils, as a means of determining promotion or failure. These are not the significant purposes of an adequate testing programme. Evaluation seeks to determine the quality and amount of student development. It has a broader connotation than measurement in appraising the consequences of one's teaching efforts.

Evaluation is a qualitative process dealing with a wide range of human activity, such as achievements, attitudes and interests. It is the process of stock-taking. Appraisal of all outcomes of learning, both quantitative and qualitative, is included in the concept of evaluation. The evaluation of physical education practices must be in terms of their effects. As Lockhart would put it, "Results must be planned for; to be convincing, they must be shown". If we really heeded the five requirements for a successful physical education programme, we would lessen our present trend toward confusion and more in the direction of more consistency of action by insisting upon the following:

i. A sound philosophy and measurable objectives.

ii. A realistic curriculum which translates the philosophy into experiences to achieve the objectives.

iii. Good class organization and teaching methods to implement the curriculum.

iv. An evaluation programme to appraise achievement.

v. An interpretation and reporting programme to inform the public.

Parents, pupils, taxpayers and school administrators should insist upon results from a physical education programme. To indicate results, some means of measuring the change in the status of pupils is imperative. Sometimes physical education programmes are difficult to sell because the claims for them are difficult to prove. While evaluation seeks to determine the quality and amount of student development and is the more inclusive determination of amount, which quantity, with the focus. How much does the child know?

How far or how high can he jump? What is his grip strength? Although measurements are the raw data for evaluation, the two terms are not synonymous.

For evaluation, tools, techniques or instruments are needed. These range from standardized tests to observational judgements. The first step in evaluation is to formulate in clear and understandable fashion the major purposes of the physical education programme. We must indicate the changes in pupils we expect to facilitate. We must ask, "What do we expect to result from this activity?" Unless objectives really make a difference in what we do as teachers, their formulation is simply a waste of time. We should think of objectives as the directions in which we are trying to change pupils. Each physical education department must clarify its own objectives and formulate its underlying philosophy in clear and consistent terms. It must critically examine its own practices, determine the foundations upon which they are based and commit itself with respect to fundamental issues, of which today there are many. Some rather specific purposes of evaluation are:

i. To help teachers, parents, and pupils examine the values they want to achieve from the physical education programme.

ii. To give strong encouragement to administrators, teachers, parents, and students to evolve certain policies, blueprints of goals and direction, as basic agreements of educational purposes against which to validate their educational procedures.

iii. To provide a periodic check on the degree to which specified objectives are attained for an individual or group of individuals.

iv. To improve counselling methods by providing basic

information and new insight into the needs of individual students.

v. To encourage teachers to adjust and improve the teaching process and methods to aid in the achievement of objectives.

vi. To give administrators, teachers, parents and students certain psychological security and a feeling of accomplishment.

vii. To form the basis for sound public relations by helping the taxpayer to realize that his money is contributing toward healthy and happier children today and better citizens tomorrow.

viii. To stimulate greater professional growth in teachers.

The Use of Tests and Other Devices

A test is a systematic procedure for comparing the behaviour of two or more people. It is also the task that is performed as well as the method of appraising or defining an ability. We deal with proficiency tests, achievement tests and aptitude tests. Such factors as muscular strength, agility, flexibility, speed, endurance, balance, depth perception, kinesthetic memory, co-ordination, insight, and a host of other psycho-physical and psycho-social traits or individual attributes are involved. A proficiency or achievement test measures ability to perform some task which is significant in its own right, such as swimming, general motor ability, the dance, or gymnastics.

Principally, the tests are used to evaluate the performance of people who have received special training in the activities tested, hence the term achievement test. An aptitude test in physical education is one used to predict success in some future physical education activity. While an achievement test examines a person's success as a result of past physical education experience, an aptitude test is used to forecast his success in future physical education experience. A test of athletic aptitude, for example, represents present motor traits or attributes as predictors of future athletic achievement. In using the term aptitude, specific inherited aptitude is not implied. A good achievement test of strength is a predictor of future achievement in physical education performance since it measures one important aspect of physical education performance since it measures one important aspect of physical education aptitude, just as pitch discrimination is one aspect of musical ability. We deal with such outcomes as development as physical fitness, motor fitness and motor ability.

Uniformly acceptable definitions of these terms are still to be determined and in some cases will have to await further factor analysis research studies to stabilize the definitions. Motor fitness is a state of general physical efficiency. It is a state of adaptability or possession of traits which enable one to be efficient in muscular movement. The chief criterion of motor fitness is the ability to perform motor activities with physical efficiency, skill, and competence. Motor fitness and motor ability are rather difficult to isolate separately in terms of definition. Fitness implies the state of adaptability or possession of attributes or traits. Ability represents the power to perform.

Physical fitness is best defined in terms of work capacity, and this is what we test either directly or indirectly by the several variables we employ in a battery of test items.

As educators, we are not interested merely in physical education skills and organic power but in what happens to human personality as a result of these, evaluation must include appraisal of personality development, interests, attitudes and other aspects of pupil behaviour. If we accept education as the social process of change in the behaviour of the human organism, we agree that these changes include many phases in the life of the learner and that, to be comprehensive, an evaluation programme cannot be limited to the use of tests alone. Instruments such as rating scales, anecdotal records, interest inventories, and check lists are needed. What we cannot measure, we will have to judge. We can see that, since the primary purpose of evaluation is to improve learning, evaluation must be as wide and diversified as the instructional programme.

We need not only the formal testing programme concerned with such factors as knowledge, skills, strength and endurance, but, also the informal evaluation of social development based on sociometric friendship tests and personal distance scales. Attitude scales and appraisal of character traits by rating scales and guess who techniques provide additional means of informal evaluation of important non-intellectual determiners of success. The ultimate purpose of evaluation is to establish, as objectively as possible, a comprehensive picture of each pupil's developmental growth. Evaluation should aid us in finding answers about the progress pupils are making toward the objectives, first, of the physical education programme, and secondly, toward the general objectives of the school as a whole.

Data in an evaluation programme will have value for individual guidance and curriculum revision only if thoughtful interpretations are made. Furthermore, it is difficult to draw valid conclusions from one test or disregarded in the light of evidence drawn from other sources. No one item in a record should be taken at its face value alone but always considered in relation to all other information about a pupil before an accurate picture of his various attributes can be obtained. For this reason, a graphic record of developmental growth is exceedingly helpful. Let us ask ourselves frankly, "What does an A or a D as a single mark in physical education actually mean to the teacher, the pupil, and his parents?" Surely a single mark can neither indicate the point at which the pupil needs improvements nor guide him in planning his next steps. Progress can be determined only if we have at least two evaluations, the first being the base line for reference. The pupil's present status becomes important in relation to his past performance records. The all-round growth of the pupil rather than his present status alone should be the focus of attention in any good evaluation and guidance programme.

The Relation of Physical Education to Guidance

The guidance programme in a school provides that body of services organized specifically to help pupils identify and solve their problems and improve their planning. It is not concerned with telling the student what to do or with making decisions for him, but with assisting him through component counselling, to direct his own life, develop his own point of view, and make his own decisions.

12

ORGANISATION AND ADMINISTRATION IN PHYSICAL EDUCATION

ORGANISATION

The word organisation has two meaning. In one sense, it is used as an association like Taj Group of Hotels Organisation, Young Men's Christian Association (Y.M.C.A.), Young Women's Christian Association) Y.W.C.A.), W.H.O. (World Health Organisation) etc. The other meaning of the word organisation is "Setting up of things". Organisation is a plan of work. It helps towards proper working of the institute.

It is the process which arranges all the elements of particular enterprise into systematic way so that the whole setting works as a unit.

Without proper organisation no institute can work effectively.

In order to run an institution efficiently and effectively a well-knit organisation and expert administration is required for the smooth functioning of different activities. An organization is a social arrangement which pursues collective goals, which controls its own performance, and which has a boundary separating it from its environment. The word itself is derived from the Greek word 'Organon' meaning tool.

The term is used in both daily and scientific English in multiple ways. In the social sciences, organizations are studied by researchers from several disciplines, the most common of which are sociology, economics, political science, psychology, management, and organizational communication. The broad area is commonly referred to as organizational studies, organizational behaviour or organization analysis. Therefore, a number of different theories and perspectives exist, some of which are compatible, and others that are competing.

Organization – process-related: an entity is being organized. Organization – functional: organization as a function of how entities like businesses or state authorities are used (organization as a permanent structure).

Organization – institutional: an entity is an organization. Organisation gives existence to an institution and administration executes its plans and takes it to the desired goals. Without these significant aspects no institution can work well. Education aims at all-round development of an individual's personality. In order to achieve this very aim it is essential for an educational institution or school to provide different activities to its students. Its activities are not limited only to the classroom teaching but extend to provision of sports, recreation, physical education, health, beautification of schools and its surroundings etc. Successful and effective provision of all these activities needs well planned organisation and skilful administration.

ADMINISTRATION

The meaning of the word 'Administration' is perform, take charge or accomplish. It is a process of functioning or working the planned organisation. That process of functioning and operation of organisation is administration.

Organisation and administration are closely related. They are in separable. They are inter-dependent. Though they are not synonymous.

Administration is to get the work done properly. To see that the functioning of an institution is going smoothly, effectively in a desired way. There is really a great need of organisation and administration in providing different activities in a school.

Administrator can serve as the title of the general manager or company secretary who reports to a corporate board of directors. This title is archaic, but, in many enterprises, this function, together with its associated Finance, Personnel and management information systems services, is what is intended when the term "the administration" is used.

In some organisational analyses, management is viewed as a subset of administration, specifically associated with the technical and mundane elements within an organization's operation. It stands distinct from executive or strategic work.

In other organizational analyses, administration can refer to the bureaucratic or operational performance of mundane office tasks, usually internally oriented and reactive rather than proactive.

Administrators, broadly speaking, engage in a common set of functions to meet the organization's goals. These "functions" of the administrator were described by Henri Fayol.

Planning is deciding in advance what to do, how to

do it, when to do it, and who should do it. It maps the path from where the organization is to where it wants to be. The planning function involves establishing goals and arranging them in logical order. Administrators engage in both short-range and long-range planning.

Organizing involves identifying responsibilities to be performed, grouping responsibilities into departments or divisions, and specifying organizational relationships. The purpose is to achieve coordinated effort among all the elements in the organization. Organizing must take into account delegation of authority and responsibility and span of control within supervisory units.

Staffing means filling job positions with the right people at the right time. It involves determining staffing needs, writing job descriptions, recruiting and screening people to fill the positions.

Directing is leading people in a manner that achieves the goals of the organization. This involves proper allocation of resources and providing an effective support system. Directing requires exceptional interpersonal skills and the ability to motivate people. One of the crucial issues in directing is to find the correct balance between emphasis on staff needs and emphasis on economic production.

Controlling is the function that evaluates quality in all areas and detects potential or actual deviations from the organization's plan. This ensures high-quality performance and satisfactory results while maintaining an orderly and problem-free environment. Controlling includes information management, measurement of performance, and institution of corrective actions.

Budgeting, exempted from the list above, incorporates most of the administrative functions, beginning with the implementation of a budget plan through the application of budget controls.

BASIC PRINCIPLES OF ORGANISATION AND ADMINISTRATION

Physical Education is gaining more and more importance in educational institutions. It is essential that it should be effectively organised and administered. It necessities that basic principles of organisation and administration should be followed while organising physical activities in the school. These basic principles are as under:-

1. Human Base

Organisation and administration of physical education should be based on the principles of humanity, because it is concerned with the all-round development of the students. To think students as machines is the greatest blunder. Similarly, they should not be treated as animals. Human behaviour with the students will attract them towards physical education and they will start taking keen interest in different kinds of physical activities.

2. Organisation of Human Elements

No activity of school can be organised without human elements. For useful administration of physical education related human elements should be organised properly and effectively. It is true that in organising physical education, physical instructor plays the leading role because he is trained for the same, but he along can not plan and organise such a big job. He needs active co-operation of other teachers and headmaster.

3. Co-operation of Guardians

Guardians of the students should also be made to take

interest in the programmes of physical education. To create their interest, it is essential that their active co-operation should be sought. It is generally believed that while organising physical activities the aptitudes, interests and physical capabilities of students must be kept in mind. Co-operation of guardian enables them to keep close contact with the school and prove conducive in solving various problems of the student.

4. Co-operation and Co-ordination

No physical activity can be organised without co-operation and co-ordination. Whole function of physical education is divided into different sub-activities. These sub-activities are assigned to different teachers according to their interest and abilities. Now if there is no co-ordination among these sub-activities, whole programme of physical education will remain scatter.

5. Exchange of Thought

Before planning any activity of the school, it is essential that it should be discussed thoroughly from every angle. Discussion should continue from beginning to the end of the programme. Without proper discussion no activity can be justified. Participation in discussion builds up confidence and interest.

6. Clear and Good Administration

For successful organisation of any activity in school, clear and good administration is a must. It means that aims and objective of that activity should be clean and well-defined. The rules, regulations and procedure to be followed should be definite and clear. Good administration also demands that talent of the students should be given due recognition and favouritism should not be shown to any body.

7. Elasticity in Organisation and Administration

Mind and brain of these organisms is under various kinds of influences and elasticity of organisation and administration is very essential to strike harmony with these influences. This elasticity is all the more essential in organisation and administration of physical education activities because these activities are organised in open grounds where sudden weather changes have to be taken into consideration and programmes be changed accordingly.

8. Need of Self-governing

The student must be active participants in organisation and administration of any activity in school. Activities must be organised on the basis of self-government to develop the qualities of leadership and co-operation in the students.

9. Organisation and Administration is a means, not an end

It should be borne in mind that various activities are organised and administered to reach some definite goals. Organisation and administration is not an end. It is only the medium by which a desired goal is achieved. The main aims of various activities of physical education is development of health, character and personality of the students.

Organisation and Administration is not an end. It is the progress of students' life. The aims and objectives of the physical activities is must be fulfilled by the appropriate organisation and administration.

GUIDING PRINCIPLES OF ORGANISATION AND ADMINISTRATION

Some fundamental principles are to be kept in mind while organising any activity of physical education. For example, principle of human base, organisation and use of human elements, co-operation of guardians, co-operation and co-ordination between organisation and participants, elasticity of organisation and proper use of equipment etc. But these principles are not sufficient since they only form the foundation on which the organisation of various activities rests.

But the success, usefulness and popularity of a programme depends upon the guiding principles.

These principles are stated as below: -

1. Biological need of children

Physical education fulfils the biological needs of the children. The various physical activity in the programme should be organised and administered in such a manner that the biological need of the participants is fulfilled. Otherwise, organisation of activity will be a useful act.

2. Physical Education—A Daily Necessity

Regular physical activity is necessary for a sound, active, well-developed personality. Physical education renders a great help in making a sound body and mind through daily physical activity.

3. In accordance with student's interest

Student's interest in the activity should also be considered. He/she should be allowed to take part in the game, sports, activity or his choice so that he can bring name and fame for institution and for him. So, physical education activities must be organised in accordance with the student's interest.

4. According to Student's Ability

Physical activity is a daily need. Regular activity brings healthy, sound, smart students. Every student must participate in physical activities for their mental and physical development. Hence, it is necessary that physical activities be so organised that every student can take part according to his abilities.

5. Facilities available

Organisation of every activities in school must be done while keeping the available facilities in mind. Otherwise, lack of facilities will make a sound organisation a big flop.

6. Provision of Funds

Money is the most important aspect in any organisation and administration. A sufficient sports fund must be provided while planning the annual budget of school. Physical education programmes must be organised within provided financial limits.

7. Importance of Natural Activity

Students are particularly interested in natural body movements. It is better and is necessary too, that natural body movements are given their proper place in the physical education programmes.

8. Teaching in small groups

Students must be divided into small groups and time-table should be planned accordingly. Students are understand very well. Teacher learn very well and control. Maintain the discipline.

9. Education of Whole Man

Our educational system aims at all round and complete development of personality from all points of view - physical, mental and cultural. Physical education should be all-round development of the student.

10. Provision of Recreation

Recreation holds an important place in life. It relieves man of his mental, tensions and worries. Recreation refreshes a tired student immensely. Some activities are full of enjoyment in themselves. For instance Picnic, sports organise, folk songs and folk dances.

11. Proper allotment of time

Organisation and administration of various activities in physical education will not bear result if each activity is not allotted a proper and sufficient time. Sport competition must be organised depending upon time available.

12. Variety of Activities

Variety of activities is takes a big place in our physical education programme. Each student can participate according to his interest and ability. Only organisation of a number of activities can fulfil physical, mental and intellectual needs of the students.

13. Need of individual attention

It is depend on the teaching learning process. For the successful function of physical education programme, every student should be given individual attention.

14. Economical Planning

Good economic condition is very essential to planning any organisational programme. Principle of economic planning should also be kept in mind while organising programmes of physical education.

15. Special Training to Talented Student

To start special training for extra-ordinary student, such talented students should be identified and every efforts should be made to develop their talent.

16. An integrated programme of physical education

Programme of physical education should be chalked out on integrated basis. Integrated programme will also increase the popularity of physical education.

17. Evaluation

What are the results of physical education programme. To know this, evaluation of programme is very essential. Evaluation also points out the flows in the programme. Thus, evaluation helps in making the future programmes better and more effective. Organisation of physical education programmes will also create new awakening among the students and the public towards the need of physical education.

CHIEF ELEMENTS OF ORGANISATION AND ADMINISTRATION

Various activities of schools cannot be properly organized and administered without knowledge of various elements of organization and administration. These elements are as follows:-

(i) Staff

There is no doubt that whole functioning of a school depends upon Headmaster but he cannot do all the activities by himself. He is helped by teachers. Since all teachers cannot do all works, it is necessary that assignments must be made according to taste, aptitude and ability of the teachers. Number of persons required to organize an activity must be assessed before commencing the work and persons must be assigned duties according to their ability. It is worth remembering that no activity– especially Physical Education activities– can produce desired results without able and sufficient staff.

(ii) Material Equipment

Some equipment is needed for the planning and organization of an activity. Organisers and administrators must have proper and extensive knowledge of this equipment and it must be made available for the activity.

(iii) Allocation of Work

As said before, proper administration is not possible without able and sufficient staff. Besides take the taste of the person into consideration while assigning a work, it is also necessary that work should be allocated evenly. It must be borne into mind that no one should be allocated more work than others.

(iv) Direction

Every activity in school must be under control of one person. This person have complete knowledge about the organization and administration of that activity. He should also direct the activity. Direction is not synonymous with ordering. It means the taking over of the activity towards desired goal with the help of others. Direction must be according to the situation. Director should do his work while keeping the feelings of co-operation and goodwill in his mind.

(v) Co-ordination

Every activity is divided into many parts or sub-activities for its strong organization and smooth administration. For instance, plan of physical education is divided into theoretical teaching, practicals and competitions. Co-ordination between various sub-activities is very essential. Without co-ordination, organization and administration cannot be effective, useful and result-bearing.

(vi) Report and Record

Report of every activity in school must be prepared and sent to higher officials. It is also very necessary that report must be safely put in school record since it gives an indication of school's progress. It also helps in administration and organization of same activity in future.

RELATIONSHIP OF ORGANISATION AND ADMINISTRATION WITH PHYSICAL EDUCATION

Physical education holds an important position in modern educational system. No doubt, complete development is impossible without a sound body. Health and physical education is also important from national social point of view. Our youth cannot be steered towards the pursuit of national development till this subject of health and physical education is properly taught in our school. According to H.D. Bucke "A properly directed physical education should result in health, happiness, efficiency and character." While describing the importance of physical education, Secondary Education Commission said, "The physical welfare of youth of the country should be one of the main concerns of state and any departure from the normal standards of physical well being at this period of life may have serious consequence." For this very reason, physical education has been included in the syllabi of schools.

Physical education must be properly organized and effectively administered to achieve the desired aims. These aims are as follows:-

(A) Maintenance of health.

(B) Development of well built body.

(C) Making of a sound personality by physical development.

(D) Development of individual qualities like self-control tolerance and courage etc.

(E) Prevention of disease.

(F) Development of social qualities like co-operation, obedience and goodwill.

(G) Development of regular habits of sports and Physical exercise.

For the achievement of above mentioned aims, the programme of physical education is sub-divided into many parts such as:

(i) Theoretical teaching
(ii) Practical teaching
(iii) Teaching ability
(iv) Officiating ability

Well-knit organization and administration are the primary needs for the programmes to be effective. Although physical education comes under the general organization and administration of school, it is imperative that special attention must be given to it for reaching the desired goal. All the above given activities of physical education are closely related to each other. Although each is properly organized and controlled by separate officials, co-ordination between them is very essential. From administration point of view, each part of physical education programme is divided into various departments which are controlled by their own heads. Their working is inspected and directed by a head administrator. He sees to it that working of one department should not hinder the activities of other departments.

In other words, he ensures co-ordination between different departments for a common motive. Whole programme of physical education cannot run smoothly unless it is properly organized and effectively administered. It is clear that physical education is closely related with organization and administration. It is a worth remembering fact that organization and administration are only the medium. It is wrong to consider them an end. Caution must be kept that organization and administrative procedures should not hinder the programme itself. These must be elastic so that these can be changed as per necessity. Aims of physical education is end and their medium–organization and administration–can be changed according to need.

13

INTRAMURAL COMPETITION AND EXTRAMURAL COMPETITIONS

This present study is concerned with a second component, the intramural, extramural and club phase of the physical education program. This component offers competitive and other types of physical activities for individuals of all levels of skills and abilities. Intramurals and extra-murals comprise that phase of a physical education program in a school, college, industry, or other organization geared to the abilities and skills of the entire student body or the members of the organization. It consists of voluntary participation in games, sports, and other activities.

This phase offers intramural activities within a single school or other institution and such extramural activities as play and sports day that bring together participants from several institutions. A club program is usually devoted to one activity such as tennis, skiing, or mountain climbing, and it encourages students and other individuals to participate at all levels of skill. It may be managed by members of an organization, such as students in schools and colleges, or by the central management of an organization. Members, advisors, or community volunteers provide instruction. Clubs are popular in schools and colleges, as well as in other organizations.

RELATION TO BASIC INSTRUCTIONAL AND HIGHLY ORGANIZED ATHLETIC PROGRAMS

Intramural and extramural activities and interscholastic and intercollegiate athletics are integral phases of the total physical education program in a school or college, which consists of the instructional program, the adapted program, the intramural and extramural program, and the varsity athletic program. Each has an important contribution to make to the achievement of physical education objectives. It is important to maintain a proper balance so each phase enhances and does not restrict the other phases of the total program. The basic instructional program in physical education is looked on by most physical education leaders as the foundation on which the adapted, intramural and extramural, and highly organized athletic programs rest.

The instructional program includes teaching such things as concepts, skills, and strategies. Intramural, extramural, and club programs provide opportunities for students and others to use these concepts, skills, and strategies in games and contests that are usually competitive. This part of the total physical education program is often referred to as the laboratory where the individual has an opportunity to experiment and test what has been learned in the instructional program. Whereas intramurals and extra-murals are for everyone, varsity athletics are usually for those individuals skilled in various physical activities.

INTRAMURAL AND EXTRAMURAL PROGRAMS

Health

Intramural and extramural activities contribute to the physical, social, and emotional health of the individual. They contribute to physical health through participation in activities offering healthful exercise.

Such characteristics as strength, agility, speed, and body control are developed. They contribute to social health through group participation and work toward achievement of group goals. They contribute to emotional health by helping a person achieve self-confidence and improve his or her self concept.

Objectives

The objectives of intramural and extramural programs are one indication of why such programs have expanded greatly throughout the country. The objectives of intramural and extramural activities are compatible with the overall objectives of physical education and also with those of education in general. The objectives of the intramural and extramural programs may be classified under four headings: (1) health, (2) skill, (3) social development, and (4) recreation.

Social Development

Opportunities for social development are numerous in intramural and extramural activities. Through many social contacts, coeducational experiences, playing on teams, and other situations, desirable qualities are developed. Individuals group and to develop sportsmanship; they also learn fair play, courage, group loyalty, social poise, and other desirable traits. Voluntary participation exists in such a program, and persons who desire to play under such conditions will live by group codes of conduct. These experiences offer training for citizenship, adult living, and human relations.

Skills

Intramural and extramural activities offer the opportunity for every individual to display and develop his or her skills in various physical education activities. Through specialization and voluntary participation they offer people the opportunity to excel and to experience the thrill of competition. It is generally agreed that an individual enjoys activities in which he or she has developed skill. Participation in athletics offers the opportunity to develop proficiency in group activities where each person is equated according to skill, thus providing for equality of competition, which helps guarantee greater success and enjoyment. Intramurals also enable many persons to spend leisure moments profitably and happily.

POLICIES FOR ORGANIZATION AND MANAGEMENT

A list of policies governing the various features of the program should be in writing and well publicized, perhaps as a handbook. Policies for intramurals and extra-murals should be developed in at least the following areas: student involvement in the organization and management of these programs, health and welfare of all participants, activities that meet the interests and needs of the participants, officiating, protests, eligibility standards, fees, postponements, point systems, and awards.

SPORTS CLUBS

The concept of a sports club originated in Europe where many community sports clubs exist. A sports club specializes in a particular activity. Club teams are often established, and equipment and other expenses are usually paid for by the club members. The administration of the club is composed of voluntary or paid coaches, managers, and officers. Some advantages of sports clubs include the following: they provide opportunities for students and others to engage in activities of interest to them but not available in other parts of the physical education program; they provide opportunities for self-administration, self-financing, and self-planning; and they provide opportunities for self-administration, self-financing, and self-planning; and they provide opportunities for students and faculty members to participate together.

MANAGEMENT PERSONNEL

Many management personnel are needed if an intramural and extramural program is to be a success. Some key persons involved are the director, student leaders, student directors and unit managers, intramural and extramural council members, and officials.

Student Leaders

Student involvement in all phases of education has been steadily increasing. Involvement in the management of intramurals and extra-murals is happening in high schools and on college campuses. Roles of student leaders may range from serving as officials to being managers and office assistants. For example, many colleges have "drop-in" centres where student supervisors are available to establish programs, reserve equipment, and arrange for the gymnasium or swimming pool to be open for additional hours. Some schools have student managers who supervise intramural activity.

Officials

Excellent officials are necessary for a sound intramural program. They should have special qualifications, including a knowledge of the activity, the participants, the goals of the program, and the organization's philosophy of competition. Some of the responsibilities of the managers of the intramural program are to find sources for good officials and then to select and train them so they enhance the program. Some of the duties performed by officials are to have game equipment ready before the contest, see that accurate score sheets accurate score sheets are prepared, check for any safety hazards, prepare accident reports if needed, and officiate the game or activity objectively and impartially.

The Director

Many larger schools, colleges, business, and other organizations have established the position of director of intramurals and extra-murals. In some cases other titles are used. The director is responsible for establishing programs, getting adequate funding, involving the community, and evaluating the success of the program. Some of the more specific duties of the director include planning programs; organizing tournaments and other forms of competition; supervising the maintenance of facilities, equipment, and supplies; attending and planning intramural council meetings; interpreting the program to the membership, the management, and the public in general; supervising the program in action; preparing budgets; and evaluating the worth of the program.

Intramural and extramural council members

An important feature of the overall management of an intramural or extramural program is an intramural and extramural council, which is usually an elected council with representatives from the participants, central administration, intramural staff, health department, and staff. The council is influential in establishing policy and practices for a broad athletic program.

The council assists and advises the person in charge and the staff members. In some cases it plays an important role in the decision-making process. Councils usually have representatives from the various participating units who communicate information to the participating teams.

ORGANIZATIONAL CONSIDERATIONS

The organization of an intramural or extramural program involves selecting activities, scheduling, determining eligibility, establishing awards and point systems, maintaining records, planning health examinations, financing, and directing publicity and promotion.

Scheduling

The time when intramural and extramural activities are scheduled will depend on the facilities, season of year, community, facility availability, student needs, and budget requirements. One of the most popular and convenient times for schools is late afternoon. This has proved best for many elementary, junior high, and senior high schools. In the spring and fall it has also been popular in colleges.

It is an economical time because lights are not required and the outdoors is available. It also ensures more faculty supervision. Evenings have been used quite extensively at colleges during the winter. This is not recommended for elementary, junior high, or senior high schools. Some schools use hours during the schools day. The physical education class is primarily an instructional period, however, and use of this period for intramurals or extra-murals does not seem to be in conformance with the standards set by the profession. However, some schools have satisfactorily used free periods, activity periods, and club periods for the program when facilities are available.

Activities

The activities constituting the intramural and extramural program determine the amount of resulting participation. It is therefore important to select the right activities. Some management guidelines that will help in selecting activitics follow:

1. Activities should reflect the needs and interests of the students of the members of the organization.

2. The activities included in the physical education school instructional program should be coordinated with the activities included in the intramural and extramural program. The latter should act as a laboratory for the former.

3. Consideration should be given to such recreational activities as field trips, dramatics, hiking, and handicrafts.

4. Activities should be selected in accordance with the season of the year and local conditions and influences.

5. Coeducational recreational activities should be provided.

6. Activities should be selected with special attention to the ability and safety of the participant.

Self-directed intramural activities should have a place. Opportunities should be provided for students to come to a facility and work out without having to enter a competitive tournament. This is particularly necessary in light of the physical fitness movement and today's busy life-style. The following are some activities that have been used successfully in various intramural and extramural programs throughout the nation:

Selected team sports

Baseball, Softball, Basketball, Speedball, Field hockey, Swimming, Foctball, Touch football, Gymnastics, Track and field, Ice hockey, Volleyball, Lacrosse, Water games, Soccer.

Selected recreational activities

Camping and cookouts, Hostelling, Canoeing, Ice skating, Cycling, Rifle, Dancing, Roller skating, Figure skating, Rowing, Fishing, Sailing, Hiking, Sailing, Horseback riding, Tumbling.

Selected individual activities

Archery, Racquet-ball, Badminton, Rope climbing, Billiards, Scuba diving, Bowling, Shooting, Curling, Shuffleboard, Cycling, Skiing, Deck tennis, Swimming, Golf, Table tennis, Gymnastics, Tennis, Handball, Track and field, Horseshoes, Tumbling, Paddle tennis, Weight lifting, Physical fitness, Wrestling.

Awards

There are arguments pro and con concerning granting awards for intramural and extramural competition. Some argue that awards stimulate interest, are an incentive for participation, and recognize achievement. Some argue that awards make the program more expensive, that a few individuals win most of the awards, and that they are unnecessary because individuals would participate even if no awards were given. Leaders who oppose awards also stress that there should be no expectation of awards for voluntary, leisure-time participation and that it is difficult to make awards on the basis of all factors that should be considered.

Eligibility

A few simple eligibility rules are needed. These should be kept to a minimum, because the intramural and extramural programs should offer something for the vast majority of students. It is generally agreed that in schools and colleges players should not be allowed to participate in activities when they are on the varsity team or squad. Professionals should be barred from those activities in which they are professional. A student should be allowed to participate on only onc team in a given activity during the season.

Students, of course, should be regularly enrolled in the school and carrying what the institution rules in a normal load. Unsportsmanlike conduct should be dealt with in a manner that is in the best interests of the individual concerned, the program, and the established goals. Certain activities by their very nature should not be engaged in by individuals with certain health problems. Therefore such individuals should be cleared by the health department of the school before participation is allowed in such activities. Recently, several states have instituted policies linking academic achievement and attendance of students with their eligibility to participate in extracurricular activities. However, some controversy has developed about whether a student should be denied the right to participate in such activities because of low grades. In some cases state officials have threatened to challenge such action in the court.

Point systems

Most intramural programs have a cumulative point system figured on an all-year basis, which maintains interest and enthusiasm over the course of the school year and encourages greater participation. A system of keeping points should be developed that stimulates wholesome competition, maintains continued interest, and is in conformance with the objectives of the total program. The system should be readily understood by all easy to administer. Under such conditions, points should be awarded on the basis of contests won, championships gained, standing in a league or order of finishing, participation, sportsmanship, and contribution to the objectives of the program.

Publicity and promotion

Members of an organization and the public and general must understand the intramural and extramural programs, the individuals they service, the activities offered, and their objectives. Such information can be disseminated to the right individuals only through a well-planned publicity and promotion program. Newspapers should be encouraged to give appropriate space to these activities. Brochures, bulletin boards, posters, and the school or organization's newspaper can help focus attention on the program. Notices can be prepared and sent home to parents in elementary and secondary schools.

MANAGEMENT CONCERNS IN ELEMENTARY AND SECONDARY SCHOOLS

The management of intramurals at the elementary and secondary school levels presents some problems that are peculiar to these programs. Whereas in many colleges and universities students live in dormitories and on campus, this is not the case in elementary and secondary schools. Some students in the lower educational levels have to work after school or catch a bus to take them home and cannot stay after school to participate in intramurals, whereas the college student more often is able to participate because he or she is not faced with such a problem, at least in institutions where dormitory living exists. Also, many times the parents of elementary and secondary school students do not see the value of intramurals and so do not have their sons and daughters participating in them after school. College students, on the other hand, make their own decisions in most cases. Another problem faced by managers of elementary and secondary school intramural programs is the unavailability of facilities. Most schools have only one gymnasium and limited outdoor space. Varsity sports often are given priority in the use of these facilities, which work a hardship on the intramural program.

PATTERNS OF ORGANIZATION

Intramural and extramural programs in the middle school and junior high school

The main concentration in athletics should be on intramurals in the middle school and intramurals and extra-murals in the junior high school. At these educational levels students are taking a special interest in sports, but at the same time their immaturity makes it unwise to allow them to engage in a highly organized interscholastic program. The program should involve both boys and girls, appeal to the entire student body, have good supervision by a trained physical educator, and be adapted to the need and interests of the pupils. Many authoritative and professional groups favour broad intramural and extramural programs and oppose a varsity interscholastic, competitive program in junior high school.

They feel this is in the best interests of youths at this age. The junior high school provides a setting for giving students fundamental skills in many sports and activities. It is a time of limitless energy when physiological changes and rapid growth are taking place. Youths in junior high schools should have proper outlets to develop themselves healthfully.

Intramural and extramural programs in other organizations

Intramural and extramural programs play a major role in many organizations outside the educational domain. For example, in industry there are many intramural leagues for employees in a variety of sports and other physical activities. In many instances baseball diamonds, basketball courts, jogging areas, platform and lawn tennis courts, swimming pools, and even golf courses are provided.

Intramural and extramural programs in the elementary school

The intramural and extramural programs in the elementary school should be outgrowth of the instructional program. They should consist of a broad variety of activities including stunts, rhythmic activities, relays, and tumbling. They should be suited to the ages and interests of children at this level and should be carefully supervised. The younger children in the primary grades probably will benefit most from free play. In the upper elementary grades, recess periods and after school activities can take place on both intragrade and intergrade bases.

The programs should be broad, varied, and progressive, with participants similar in maturity and ability. Guidelines for intramural and extramural programs in the elementary school follow:

1. Qualified leadership should be provided, including competencies involving understanding the physical, mental, emotional, and social needs of elementary school children.

2. Intramurals and extra-murals should be limited to grades four through six in the elementary school. In grades kindergarten through three the regular basic instructional physical education program provides sufficient competition.

3. Activities such as tackle football and boxing should not be permitted.

Intramural and extramural programs in the senior high school, college, and university

At senior high schools, colleges, and universities the

intramural and extramural programs should receive a major emphasis. At this time the interests and needs of students require such a program. These students want and need to experience the joy and satisfaction that are a part of playing on a team, excelling in an activity with one's own peers, and developing skill. Every high school, college, and university should see to it that a broad and varied program is part of the total physical education plan. The intramural and extramural programs should receive more emphasis than they are now getting at senior high schools and colleges.

They are basic to sound education. They are settings where the skills learned and developed in the instructional program can be put to use in a practical situation, with all the fun that comes from such competition. They should from a basis for applying skills that will be used during leisure time, both in the present and in the future. Personnel for such programs should be adequate. Good leadership is needed if the programs are to prosper. Each school should be concerned with developing a plan where proper supervision and leadership are available for after school hours. Qualified officials are also a necessity to ensure equal and sound competition.

FACULTY, STAFF, AND FAMILY PROGRAMS

Faculty members, staff members, and families of members of educational institutions and other organizations need to have opportunities to engage in recreational activities. In some institutions programs that include activities such as volleyball, softball, basketball, tennis, golf, handball, Racquet-ball, badminton, swimming, jogging, and bowling have been very popular. Sometimes teams and leagues are organized to add variety to the competition. Faculty sports clubs and fitness programs have been exceptionally well received. Faculty-family recreation nights or Saturday or Sunday afternoons are favourites.

In such cases children usually are not admitted unless accompanied by their parents. Faculty-student activities and sports nights are also scheduled in some schools and colleges. In institutions where the faculty members, staff members, and families have been provided for in the recreational program, dividends have accrued for these programs in the form of support and financial help. Participants greatly appreciate it if dressing and locker room facilities can also be furnished.

UNITS AND TYPES OF COMPETITION

The careful selection of appropriate units and types of competition will help enhance the values that accrue from intramural and extramural activities.

Types of competition

Several different ways of organizing competition are possible. Three of the most common are leagues, tournaments, and meets. These methods of organization take many forms, with league play popular in the major sports, elimination tournaments used to a great extent after league play has terminated, and meets held to culminate a season or year of sports activity. Individual and group competition may be provided. Individual competition is adaptable to such team activities as basketball, softball, and field hockey. Various types of tournament competition have been written up widely in books specializing in intramurals and other aspects of sports.

For this reason only a brief discussion of these items will be included here. The round robin tournament is probably one of the most widely used and one of the best types of competition, because it allows for maximum play. It is frequently used in leagues, where it works best with no more than eight teams. Each team plays every other team at least once during the tournament. Each team continues to play to the completion of the tournament, and the winner is the one who has the highest percentage, based on wins and losses, at the end of scheduled play. The elimination tournament does not allow for maximum play; the winners continue to play, while the losers drop out.

Units of competition

Many ways exist for organization competition for the intramural and extramural programs. The units of competition should lend interest, create enthusiasm, and allow for identity with some group where an esprit de corps can be developed and where a healthy attitude is added to the competition. At the elementary school level, the classroom provides a basis for such activity. It may be desirable in some cases to organize on some other basis, but the basic structure of the home-room lends itself readily to this purpose. At middle, junior high, and senior high schools, several units of organization are possible.

Organization may be by grades or classes, home-rooms, age, height, weight, clubs, societies, residential districts, physical education classes, study groups, or the arbitrary establishment of groups by staff members. The type of unit organization will vary from school to school and from community to community. The staff member in charge of the program should try to determine the method of organization best suited to the local situation. At a college or university or in an industry or other organization several units for organization are also possible.

EXTRA-MURALS

Extra-murals are a part of the total physical education program that represent an increase in the intensity of competition above that of intramurals. Whereas intramurals are conducted within a school, college, or other organization, extra-murals represent informal competition with other schools, colleges, and organizations. Extra-murals usually involve participants regardless of their skills and abilities. Also, they are less highly organized than varsity athletic programs. Furthermore, the emphasis is more on social outcomes than on winning. Three types of extra-murals are discussed here: sports, days, play days, and invitation days.

Sports days, play days, and invitation days

Sports days, play days, and invitation days are rapidly growing in popularity and deserve a prominent place in the extramural athletic program of any school, college, or other organization. Although they have been used mainly by girls' and women's physical education programs, they are equally important for boys and men. They have received the endorsement of AAHPERD, the National Association for Girls and Women in Sport, and many other prominent associations concerned with physical education. Sports days refer to a program when one or several schools, colleges, or other organizations participate in physical education activities. They may enter several teams in various sports. When thus organized, each team is identified with the institution it represents. Sports days may also be used to culminate a season of activity for participants within, for example, the same school or college. When several schools or colleges participate in a sports day, the number of activities may range from one to eight, although it is generally agreed that having too many activities is sometimes a disadvantage.

Play days usually refer to a day or part of a day set aside for participation in physical education activities.

It may be for participants from the same school, college, or organizations ranging from several institutions in the same community, or from many schools and colleges in various communities and organizations. In the play day each team is composed of individuals from different organizations. Here the organization loses its identity, whereas it is maintained in the sports day. The teams are usually labelled by distinctively coloured uniforms, arm bands, numbers, or some other device. The activities can be individual or team and competitive or noncompetitive. It would be noncompetitive, for example, if several students desired to engage in horseback riding, not for the purpose of competing against one another but simply for the sociability for the occasion.

Invitation days refer to a time when two schools, colleges, or other organizations usually meet for competition in an activity. This practice has worked out successfully at the end of a seasonal activity, when the winning intramural team or representatives from several teams compete against a similar group from another school, college, or other organization. The emphasis, however, it not on placing selected, highly skilled players on one team to enhance the chances of winning but on the social benefits and fun that can be gained from the occasion.

CO-EDUCATIONAL RECREATION

In light of Title IX and in view of the desire and interest on the part of girls and women to engage in sports, physical education, and recreation activities, coeducational recreation is growing very rapidly, not only in schools and colleges, but also in community recreation and other organizational programs. According to Hyatt the objectives of co-recreational sports in adapted form are as follows: (1) to provide opportunities for both sexes to engage in wholesome play experiences; (2) to provide opportunities for co-operative efforts of both sexes; (3) to provide new programs and activities for couples; (4) to enable participants to enjoy themselves, have fun, and develop friendships; (5) to provide opportunities for both sexes to experience new activities and develop skills; and (6) to provide the skills and information needed for spending leisure hours constructively in physical pursuits.

INTRAMURALS FOR THE HANDICAPPED

In the same way that instructional physical education programs are provided for the handicapped so should intramural, extramural, and club programs be provided for them. The University of New Mexico has shown how this objective can be accomplished. After assessing the needs of the handicapped at this institution it was determined that a variety of recreational activities should be available for the handicapped population on campus.

It was felt that the involvement of the handicapped in sports and related activities would be of great value to these students because they would be provided with this means of relaxation, the constructive use of leisure, and the means for maintaining good health. Next, facilities were sought that met the specialized needs of the disabled person. Then, when needed, rule modifications were made in the activities to be offered. For example, wheelchair tennis was played as doubles in the singles court, and the ball was allowed to bounce twice before being returned over the net. Sports activities at the University of New Mexico include swimming, tennis, archery, table tennis, badminton, bowling, and chess.

These activities are scheduled at the same time as the rest of the intramural program. In this way handicapped students feel a part of the regular program and social environment and at the same time the other students become aware of the needs and interests of the handicapped students. An important effort in put forth by the intramural staff members to contact personally all of the handicapped students on campus and urge them to participate in this program. Funding for such programs comes from student fees, because such fees are appropriated for all students regardless of abilities and skills.

CONCLUSION

Intramural, extramural, and club programs represent a very important component of the total physical education program. They contribute to important qualities such as skill, health, social development, and recreation. In addition, they provide an opportunity for all students to participate on a voluntary basis. Activities should be selected that reflect the basic instructional program and student interests. The management of intramurals at lower education levels is sometimes difficult because of a lack of transportation for students during after-school hours and a lack of facilities, finances, and parental support.

In order to have a well-run program the management of intramurals should be concerned with things such as scheduling, awards, point systems, eligibility requirements, and officials so that the best interests of the student and the educational process will be served. There are many different types of tournaments that can be used in intramurals to increase the flavour of the competition. Intramural programs should be evaluated periodically to determine how they can be improved to better serve the clientele for which they have been established.